Mom and Me

Lessons from God in a Bipolar World

By Effie Darlene Barba

ISBN # 978-0-9991193-5-8

Cover photo designed by RoninRon's Custom Art. You may

contact the artist at Contact@roninron.com

Unless otherwise noted, scripture is from the King James

Version Bible

So, the man who chose to follow Christ goes forward on the way. And when he must learn to know the world and what is in the world, the world's strength and his own weakness, when the struggle with flesh and blood distresses him when the going is heavy and there are many foes and no friends then the agony of it may wring from him the moan I walk alone... But on that way where a man follows Christ the height of suffering is the height of glory. Even as the pilgrim moans in his heart he reckons himself to be in bliss... And this is the joyful hope that he shall follow where He has gone.

-Soren Kierkegaard, *The Gospel of Sufferings*

Dedication to Mom

Despite a lifelong battle with bipolar disorder, Mom stood firm on this: Jesus Christ is our only hope of salvation, God's grace and love is bigger than any trial we may face, and God is the treasure our heart seeks. He is our joy, hope and peace; whatever this life brings.

Table of Contents

INTRODUCTION

But on that way where a man follows Christ the height of suffering is the height of glory.[1] (Kierkegaard) Those words ring out as a banner of truth, hope and glory for Mom. Though as a child, I did not understand the depth of trials she lived in. Nor was it something I understood, as a young woman. Even after her diagnosis of bipolar (manic depressive disorder with psychotic features), I could not fully comprehend the anguish which she faced. Oh, yes, being a nurse and later a nurse practitioner, I could tell you the medical definition. But I could not even begin to empathetically enter her world.

Instead, I found myself often frustrated by it, or angered by it at times. However, I have come to realize the strength, the courage, and the depth of love it has taken for her to live in this world. Never did her love for God falter;

---

[1] Soren Kierkegaard, *The Gospel of Sufferings,* A.S. Aldworth and W.S. Ferrie, (Cambridge, United Kingdom: James Clark & Company, 1955, 23

although, it was her lot to live a life of self-denial. Neither did her love for me ever falter. Hers has been a world of self-denial and sacrifice; hence, emulating a follower of Christ through it all. And if the height of suffering is the height of Glory, hers is a Glorious Crown awaiting her one day.

God in His Sovereign Wisdom chose Mom to be the perfect Mother, to point me to Christ as the only hope. He had through her prepared me to be the wife of Pedro Barba, Jr. Despite all my own failures, God shone forth His Light through the holes in my life to change the eternity of Pete. For you see, Pete also struggled with bipolar disorder. Many people I have met through the years have hailed my strength and courage; but alas the truth is: I have none. Mom and Pete taught me of true courage and sacrificial love. It is only through dying to self that one can one find the strength that comes from knowing Christ fully.

Perfect love is a sacrificial love as so exemplified by Jesus Christ on the cross. That kind of love, Mom demonstrated throughout my life. Although, I could not see at first the depth of her sacrifice, it was always there. For her it was a battle she silently bore within her heart and mind. Pete, also for love, ultimately sacrificed everything for me. The kind of love I could only dream of, they gave to me. If I could love with that same passion and self-sacrificing depth; I could truly know and comprehend God's love. Ah, but God is not through with me yet. He continues to transform this heart of mine day by day, until one day; I will look like Him.

Christ said, "If any man will come after me, let him deny himself, and take up his cross daily, and follow me"[2] (Luke 9:23). No one faces this truth more clearly than the Christian who suffers bipolar disorder. Theirs is a cross that wavers from self-aggrandizement to the depth of despairing self-hatred. Fears ravage their minds at times. Yet, it is there where my story begins. But it does not end there. Paul prayed that God remove the thorn in the flesh that tortured him. God's reply was: "My grace is sufficient for thee: for my

---

[2] Biblical References: Unless otherwise noted, all Biblical passages referenced are in the King James Version

strength is made perfect in weakness" (2 Corinthians 12:9). To which Paul concluded: "Most gladly therefore will I rather glory in my infirmities, that the power of Christ may rest upon me. Therefore, I take pleasure in infirmities, in reproaches, in necessities, in persecutions, in destresses for Christ's sake: for when I am weak, then am I strong" (2 Corinthians 12:9).

I Was A Child, Back Then

I was a child, back then
And did not, could not understand
The pains she faced, the fears within
Her road of life throughout this land

But as I grew I came to see
The sacrifices that she made
Because of love she had for me
No matter what it did not fade

Whatever road our feet did trod
Her courage, faith deep within
Did hold her heart so close to God
Protecting her from sin

The more I learned of God's dear Grace
Throughout the years, I came to see
The trials, sorrows that we face
Transform our hearts that we might be

1

A shining beacon on a hill

To light the path in darkest night

That strangers then might find God's will

The blinded might gain sight

Yet, each of us, God calls to be

A different beam of Glory's light

And this in part the mystery

Of how God works, that He just might

Give one the gift to speak His word

Another sings His praise

While some it seems their voice unheard

Except by God. In prayer their voices raise

Each child who knows Christ as their Lord

God uses in His own sweet way

To each He gives a different sword

His Glory Honor to display

And so, I came to realize
The chains of pride that bound my heart
Were merely part of Satan's guise
Sow bitter seeds, and then depart

I lay my "self" upon the cross
The cross where Jesus bled and died
That He might live, all else is loss
My pride He's crucified

As I look back, I now can see
That it was Mom, God used to be
A beacon of humility
His beam of Grace to shine toward me

I did not, could not understand
The pains she faced, the fears within
Her road of life throughout this land
Because I was a child, back then

Chapter 1

The Blind May See

Often illness or suffering is seen as God's punishment for sin by those who would espouse their own righteousness. A God of love would only bring abundant blessings to those who follow Him. As His Beloved, Blessed, Redeemed Child, the Christian should experience prosperity, health, and a life abounding in the joys of this world. Or so, some would say! Yet, God works in mysterious ways that our human minds cannot comprehend.

What is a life that is truly blessed? The one that is filled with all the counterfeit joys of this world? No, I dare say a thousand times no! For the one who is truly blessed is the one covered with scars, broken, unable to stand alone and finds his/her strength by falling into the arms of Christ where he/she is carried to the finish line by Christ Alone. Oh, that dear saint is the one truly blessed! Having come to the very end of one's self, one finds there a Savior who will carry him or her in His Loving Arms with an Unconditional Love and Grace that they know was wholly undeserved. Thereby making that Grace even more precious than anything else this earth could offer and their joy more miraculous than can be imagined.

THE BLIND MAY SEE

And as Jesus passed by, He saw a man which was blind from his birth. His disciples asked him, saying "Master, who did sin, this man, or his parents, that he was born blind?" Jesus answered, "Neither hath this man sinned, nor his parents: but that the works of God should be made manifest in him. I must work the works of Him that sent me, while it is day: the night cometh, when no man can work. As long as I am in the world, I am the light of the world" (John 9:5).

Jesus did not mean by this that this man nor his parents were not sinners. "For all have sinned and come short of the glory of God" (Romans 3:23). What Jesus wanted them to see was that illness, pain, and distress are not the punishment of God; rather, it can be the blessing that points one to turn to the only one who can truly save the sinner. God's Glory can only shine forth upon the one who recognizes their need of Him. Because he was born blind, this man recognized His need; whereas, the self-righteous pharisee could not. They could see the world; but, they were blind to the truth that Jesus was the light of the world, the only means to ultimately see God's Glory. Blinded by their own self-righteous pride, the Pharisees could not see God Incarnate standing in front of them as Jesus Christ, His Son. Oh, so who was truly blind-the beggar or the Pharisee?

The Plight of Mom

Was it an act of punishment that Mom was born with the genetic makeup to be bipolar or an act of God's Grace? What could possibly be God's purpose in this? How could this be His Perfect Plan of love for her? And how did He use every detail of her life to display His Glory and accomplish His will?

I doubt I can adequately answer those questions; because who can know the mind of God. (Romans 11:34). What I do know is, she pointed me to Christ. In that one act, God used her to transform my eternity. And not only I, but, my brother as well. Pedro Barba, Jr came to know Christ as his Savior before he died; therefore, stands before His throne of Grace clothed in a righteousness not his own. My three children know Jesus as Lord and Savior. So, many lives have been touched and saved; because, God touched Mom's life and her legacy of faith through trials marches on through the generations to come. That, my dear friends and readers, is God's Grace abounding in a dark world desperately in need of His light. And all of this, despite her bipolar disorder or perhaps as a part of its good. Were Mom completely whole, would she have come to know Christ. Or were it her trials that allowed her to seek Him as her Savior?

William Cowper suffered severe bouts of depression. Yet, he wrote some of the world's best hymns. His depression allowed him to seek God and to reach a depth of understanding that some may never know.

God Moves in Mysterious Ways

By William Cowper

God moves in a mysterious way

His wonders to perform;

He plants His footsteps in the sea,

And rides upon the storm.

Deep in unfathomable mines

Of never-failing skill

He treasures up His bright designs,

And works His sovereign will.

Ye fearful saints, fresh courage take,

The clouds ye so much dread

Are big with mercy, and shall break

In blessings on your head.

Judge not the Lord by feeble sense,

But trust Him for His Grace;

Behind a frowning providence

He hides a smiling face

--

His purposes will ripen fast,

Unfolding every hour;

The bud may have a bitter taste,

But sweet will be the flower.

Blind unbelief is sure to err,

And scan his work in vain;

God is His own interpreter,

And He will make it plain.[3]

---
[3] John Newton and William Cowper, *Olney Hymns,* (London, England: St. Paul's Churchyard, 1797), 255.

Bipolar Disease: Genetic or Acquired?

How much of bipolar disorder is purely a genetic makeup and how much depends upon triggering points that bring it to the forefront? I do not fully know the answer to that question. However, I do know for Mom and for Pete that there were many triggering factors. Why did God allow the suffering they endured? God does allow or even at times ordains suffering, even though He does not cause it. We know that from reading the book of Job. Sometimes, He allows it because He knows how quickly our self-exalting hearts become content with counterfeit joys, never seeking the only true joy that can be found in Him alone. Or sometimes, He ordains it that we might grow closer to Him and deeper in our faith.

God Draws Nigh to the Broken Heart

The Lord is nigh unto them that are of a broken heart; and saveth such as be of a contrite Spirit. Many are the afflictions of the righteous: but the Lord delivereth him out of them all. Psalm 34:18-19

Mom was just a little girl when her parents divorced. They decided to divide the time equally. So, mom spent six months with one and six months with the other. That meant this little girl would never complete a year in any school. Unable to truly make friends because of the constant transferring, she became very lonely.

When living with her mother, she had nicer clothes. As it is with every child, she wanted and longed for her mother's love. Often though her mother was preoccupied both with her work and her own social life. As a child, she would sometimes go to the movies only to walk home alone through the streets of Detroit to enter an empty house. Wanting to feel her mother's presence, she would sit in her mother's closet; because, there she could smell the aroma of her presence.

From Riches to Rags

Sometimes during the summer, she would be sent to her grandmother's house in Tennessee. Her grandmother was a hardworking, country lady. There was no refrigeration and meats were salt cured. The ice truck would bring around blocks of ice. Her grandfather was a bootlegger; but, her grandmother was a devote Christian who lived a life devoted to Christ.

When with her father, her clothes were less, and her life was completely different. Her step-mother was not a warm or affectionate woman, adding to mom's loneliness as a child. Although by the time I came to know my grandfather, he spoke a lot about God's grace. God had transformed his heart over the years. However, when mom was a child he was very strict and legalistic in his teaching. At least that was the impression Mom received of him and thus, of God.

A Young Broken Heart Finds Salvation

A young broken heart yearned to be loved and to find a sense of belonging. Yet, it was this young broken heart that God drew nigh. There might be years of afflictions to come; yet, through it all God had a plan. At the age of twelve, mom accepted Jesus Christ as her Savior, changing her eternity forever. God would be the anchor that steadied her through all the storms that were yet to come.

At the age of sixteen, her father, perhaps out of fear; began to tell her that her mother was a woman of ill repute. That lead to mom's first emotional breakdown. Although an excellent student, she quit school. Many years later, she got her GED; but she always regretted not finishing high school.

Ah, but history sometimes tends to repeat itself. Mom, also fearing I might sin, became the catalyst that pushed me into a horrible marriage at age 16. I did finish high school and even went on to college; but, I also started down a long road to recover from many a broken heart.

15

Mine would be a battle through many emotions: rejection, guilt, anger, and jealousy. God desired to lead me into experiencing the depth of His love and His joy. But, along that path to discovering His peace, love and joy; He would have to transform my heart one speck at a time. Each step of the way on this journey of life, from the moment I accepted Christ as my Savior at age 5, He has been steadily at work to change me into the image of Christ. He has not finished yet; but He patiently continues in this transformation process.

He longs for my heart to learn how to forgive as He does and to love with a perfect love as is His. This He desires for each of His children; because, He knows our truest joy can only be found in this. Mom and I walked this journey together. We were always more alike than I wanted to admit. Where is the line between sanity and mental illness? Sometimes, I have believed it blurred whenever I faced depression, guilt or emotional turmoil. Ah, perhaps that line is less defined than we think, and it is only a minute degree different at times.

God's Sovereign Grace

In both cases, God was there drawing nigh. He would through the years lead mom ever closer to Him. For me, God had a perfect plan through the depth of brokenness. A Broken and Contrite Heart, I wrote to tell that story back in 2010. The story tells of how a God of Grace can take all the broken pieces of one life, weave each thread together, only to create a beautiful portrait of Himself in the likeness of Jesus Christ. One Glorious day, my portrait will look like Jesus! He can take all the sorrows, the tears, the feelings of rejection, and even our failures to bring us closer to Him. There, we discover that in His presence, is fullness of joy.

Whatever broken roads we may have traveled; they led both mom and me ever closer to God. He is the rock and fortress of our lives. In His presence is fullness of joy. Furthermore, He is the greatest treasure. We may not fully comprehend the trials of this world; however, it is God's Love and Grace which allowed them all. Only He knew what it would take to not only save our soul for eternity; but, to also transform our hearts into hearts that can see glimpses of His Glory.

Now the Lord is that Spirit: and where the Spirit of the Lord is, there is liberty. But we all, with open face beholding as in a glass the glory of the Lord, are changed into the same image from glory to glory, even as by the Spirit of the Lord (2 Corinthians 3:17-18).

However, dim that view may be, or smudged the glass I look through now; I am being transformed, one tiny glory at a time into His precious image. Whatever it takes, God will perform to ascertain that truth be a reality for me and for all who know Him as Savior and Lord.

Chapter 2: Feelings of Rejection

Most of my life, I battled with feelings of rejection; somehow, feeling I never measured up. To gain God's love, I felt I must try harder. Somewhere amid the turmoil of my own mind, I believed love must be earned. A dangerous place to stand before a Holy God. My mind knew the truth of scripture; but, my heart longed to feel the reality of God's love. It would be a long road to discover the truth of God's unconditional love and grace toward me. Perhaps it was clearer, when at the age of five, I accepted Jesus Christ as my Savior. I knew then that it was grace alone that saved me. Yet, I had to learn that it is His Grace alone that loved me every step of this journey, no matter what.

There within our emotions, the battle ground lies. When facing feelings of rejection, we must first recognize it for what it is; an internal battle with the sin of pride. One of the hardest things for pride to accept is an unmerited gift. We want to believe we have earned it. Our "self" rises up to heights of aggrandizement, seeing the world through our own eyes. Yet, Christ calls us to crucify that self, so that our identity can be found in Him.

Even though on this earth, Christ faced the rejection of men, the only time He felt the weight of true rejection was when all our sin lay upon Him. The Father and Holy Spirit, unable to look upon Him, had turned their back toward Him for a second in time. For *the wages of sin is death* (Romans 6:23). Therefore, the wrath of God against sin was poured out upon Him, so that we might be redeemed. Death is separation from that which gives us life, God. Although, Himself God, Christ to pay the penalty of our sin had to be separated from God the Father and the Holy Spirit for a moment in time; thereby, experiencing death of soul and spirit. He bore no arrogance or pride, despite being the Creator of all. He never once cried out, "I don't deserve this." Instead, He humbly accepted the cross in our place. The only perfect, righteous one who did not deserve God's wrath against sin; willingly took it upon Himself so you and I would not have to. If only we would accept this gift of salvation, He purchased for us.

His is a true rejection, as those who reject the truth that He is God; whereas ours is "feelings of rejection". The truth being, God is ever reaching out to us with His love, bidding us to come to Him.

To Be Like Christ

Let nothing be done through strife or vainglory; but in lowliness of mind let each esteem other better than themselves. Look not every man on his own things, but every man also on the things of others. Let this mind be in you, which was also in Christ Jesus: Who, being in the form of God, thought it not robbery to be equal with God: But made himself of no reputation, and took upon Him the form of a

21

servant, and was made in the likeness of men: And being found in fashion as a man, He humbled Himself, and became obedient unto death, even the death of the cross. Wherefore God also hath highly exalted Him and given Him a name which is above every name: that at the name of Jesus every knee should bow, of things in heaven, and things in earth, and things under the earth; and that every tongue should confess that Jesus Christ is Lord, to the glory of God the Father (Philippians 2:3-11).

Herein lies the problem for us and why we battle these feelings of rejection. Self wants to rise upon the throne; yet, deep within we know our own sin and unworthiness, whether we admit it or not. Those feelings of unworthiness we often project onto others; so as not to bare the weight of it ourselves.

Despair Within Rejection

Soren Kierkegaard wrote in *The Sickness Unto Death,* "The self wants in its despair to savour to the full the satisfaction of making itself into itself, of developing itself, of being itself; it wants to take the credit for this fictional masterly project, its own way of understanding itself"[4]

We want to believe we deserve or have earned God's love. As such, we struggle to see that every set-back, trial, or sorrow we face are truly acts of love and grace by a Sovereign God toward us. He knows that our heart cannot find true joy, peace, and hope until it dies to self, so that He our Creator might live in and through us. This is a cross we must take up daily, for each morning "self" arises to exalt itself once more upon the throne.

Note that Christ said, "If any man will come after me, let him deny himself, and take up his cross **daily** and follow me" (Luke 9:23). Every morning we must die to self, that He might live. Ah, but it is there, when we come to the end of ourselves, that we find that abiding, steadfast joy as I described in the book I wrote by that name. All too quickly we forget

---

[4] Soren Kierkegaard, *The Sickness unto Death,* trans. Alastair Hannay (London: Penguin Books, 2004), 101.

the truths of His Sovereignty over all the details of our life. We quickly forget that His plan for us is for our ultimate joy. He desires us to remember our identity (place in this world), our purpose, and our position in Him.

Feeling Rejection, Seeking His Truth

When I forget who I am in Christ Jesus, I begin to fret and worry that perhaps His silence on answering "my requests" of Him are a sign of rejection. My mind quickly wants to pout or declare, "Maybe it is all my fault, He really doesn't love me."

Truth is I don't deserve His love; but, He loved me all the same. All He desires is to bring me to a place of fullness of joy in Him for an eternity with Him. He who created me, knows exactly what is needed to transform my heart. Therefore, whatever trial I face, He has a plan for my good.

What is my part? To seek His face every morning. Lay aside the sin of pride which so easily causes me to stumble in my faith. The more I seek Him in prayer and reading His word, the more I recognize the truth concerning His love for me. Also, I can then see that through every circumstance and trial, He is transforming me from the inside out. Something I cannot do from the outside in.

A Quasi Humility

Therefore, to deal with feelings of rejection; one must first recognize that it begins with Pride. As Christians so often declare, "I am but a sinner saved by Grace." Although this is true, all too often, it is used as a Quasi-humility. For if you and I truly grasp that truth, we could never doubt God's eternal love for us. Never would we feel as though God has rejected us nor walk around depressed over our situation, believing, God must not want to bless us. Even after we have laid our sin at the cross, our own injured pride refuses to let go of our feelings of rejection and accept the rivers of love God is pouring out upon us. We fail to recognize that everything He brings into our life is a blessing from Him.

Trying to hold onto our self-worth, we project our own feelings onto others. That way we blame someone else for our feelings of rejection. Of course, we could begin by blaming our parents. For me, that was easy. Certainly, I blamed mom for my feelings of rejection, my turmoil with wanting so desperately to be loved. Ah, but I was wrong. I could not deal with those feelings of rejection until I saw them for what they really were: my own sin of pride. You might wonder, "How can feelings of rejection be a form of pride?"

Face to Face with Pride

Let's take a moment to look at Peter when he betrayed Christ. Peter with great pride had declared that, "Even if everyone else leaves you, Jesus, I won't." (paraphrase of Matthew 26:33). Jesus told him that he, Peter would deny him three times. When Peter did deny Christ and Jesus looked at him; Peter felt the depth of remorse and believed he was now rejected by Christ. He completely forgot the remainder of what Jesus had said to him, "Simon, Simon, behold, Satan hath desired to have you, that he may sift you as wheat: But I have prayed for thee, that thy faith fail not" (Luke 22:31).

Even after all was done and he saw the resurrected Christ, Peter returned to fishing. He believed that the piercing eyes of Jesus must have now rejected him. Pride could never accept that Jesus loved him still, at least not the way He had. How could Jesus use him, a failure to lead the church? Pride could never accept that depth of forgiveness from one he betrayed!

Remember the scene at the banks when the resurrected Christ asked Peter three times, "Do you love me?" Three times, Peter responded; but, despite Christ asking, "Do you love me with an agape (God like love)? Peter's response, "I love you with a philia (friendship) love." Face to face with his own failure, Peter could not say his love was a perfect, God like love. Nor could he accept that God could love him completely and forgive him fully either. He could not forgive himself. In that, he faced his own broken, humiliated pride. Still, Christ commissioned him to "feed the sheep."

Jesus' love for Peter had not changed. His plan for Peter remained steady and sure. It was Peter, who condemned himself, not Jesus. We do the same. Whenever life gets hard or struggles come, we look within and see our own failures and wonder whether God's love remains the same. Our feelings get in the way. But the truth is, His love has not changed; because, nothing can separate us from His love. Not even our feelings of unworthiness. We were always unworthy; but, that didn't stop Jesus from dying on the cross for us.

When we lay our sins and failures at the foot of the cross, we are forgiven immediately. Our wandering around, feeling still rejected by God as though He cannot pour out His blessings on us is pride masking itself in Quasi-Humility. As though our justice is greater than God's? Our righteous indignation against ourselves is more righteous than God's? His love for us is not dependent on us. It depends upon His faithfulness, not ours. Never does His love depend upon our wavering feelings. Rather, it depends upon His unwavering covenant with all who have accepted Christ as their Savior. He is for you, not against you; if you know Jesus Christ as your Lord and Savior.

Romans 8:31-39

What shall we then say to these things? If God be for us, who can be against us? He that spared not His own Son, but delivered Him up for us all, how shall He not with Him also freely give us all things? Who shall lay anything to the charge of God's elect? It is God that justifieth. Who is he that condemneth? It is Christ that died, yea rather, that is risen again, who is even at the right hand of God, who also maketh intercession for us. Who shall separate us from the love of Christ? Shall tribulation, or distress, or persecution, or famine or nakedness, or peril, or sword?

As it is written, "For thy sake we are killed all the day long; we are accounted as sheep for the slaughter." Nay, in all these things we are more than conquerors through Him that loved us. For I am persuaded, that neither death, nor life, nor angels, nor principalities, nor powers, nor things present, nor things to come, nor height, nor depth, nor any other creature, shall be able to separate us from the love of God, which is in Christ Jesus our Lord.

Looking at Me, I Could Not See Mom

While caught up in my own feelings, I could not see that Mom also struggled with feelings of rejection. It is that way so often, you see. Our own feelings of rejection cause us to reject the person we are projecting these feelings on. Then, our actions cause them to feel rejected and a vicious cycle begins.

In her bipolar world, mom would walk into a room and believe she could hear what others were thinking. What she heard were voices rejecting and critical of her. Although these were her own thoughts about herself, it was easier to believe they came from others. She was dealing with feelings of rejection and a desperate desire to be loved.

As I began to grow in Christ and understand more about His unconditional love and grace, I should have been able to reach out to Mom and help her see the same. At moments I do; but, at other times, I fail to do that. Why? Because, I too, must each morning remind myself of who I am in Christ. Daily, I must take up my cross, die to self, and live for Christ. It is a day to day journey, seeking Him early in the morning, at moments through the day, and before I go to sleep at night. Pride and quasi humility is always lurking at the door of our hearts, for as long as we walk upon this earth. Yet, the Holy Spirit is there within us to guide us, to remind us of who we are in Christ, and to slay this dragon that would destroy us.

God's Grace Overcomes

I came face to face with my feelings of rejection when I married Pete. Believing my unworthiness, it was easy to accept the moments of abuse. Always striving to be better, wanting to gain his love; while always feeling the problem was me. Over the course of time; however, I came to realize Pete's struggles. He, too, was bipolar, although never diagnosed formally. Frightened to say, "I love you," Pete could never say the three words I so wanted to hear. He was a broken soul striving to find his way. God did an amazing thing. He filled my heart with an unconditional love that could see Pete's heart through God's eyes, leading to my staying through it all. Through all the pain, God opened my eyes to see Pete's pain. All of this, so that God through me led Pete to Christ one day shortly before he died. An eternity was changed. God taught me many lessons along that road.

God's love so great and His grace so magnificent, He used my feeble heart to be the instrument that lead Pete to Him. This life with all its years are but a split second in time compared to eternity. If filled with pains, sorrows and despair which draws one to seek God, so be it. Because nothing can compare to the joy we will know in Him. Furthermore, as we seek Him; not only will our joy be in Him one day, we also, find a place of abiding, steadfast joy here and now as we grow in our knowledge of Him.

4 Lessons from God on Rejection

1.   There is no sorrow too great to bear for the salvation of one soul.

     We need only look to Jesus to know that. As Isaiah spoke of Him.

     He is despised and rejected of men; a man of sorrows and acquainted with grief: and we hid as it were our faces from Him; He was despised, and we esteemed Him not. Surely, He hath borne our griefs, and carried our sorrows: yet we did esteem Him stricken, smitten of God, and afflicted. Isaiah 53:3-4

2.   Joy is found in a relationship with Jesus Christ, as we learn to die to self that He might live in and through us.

     I count all things but loss for the excellency of the knowledge of Christ Jesus my Lord: for whom I have suffered the loss of all things, and do count them but dung, that I may win Christ, and be found in Him, not having mine own righteousness, which is of the law, but that which is through the faith of Christ, the righteousness which is of God by faith: that I may know Him, and the power of His resurrection, and the fellowship of His sufferings, being made conformable unto His death. Philippians 3:8-10

3. Feelings of rejection are a quasi-humility born out of pride; believing we deserve more.

The truth is: in Christ Jesus we have more than we ever deserved, because of His abounding love and grace toward us.

For all have sinned and come short of the glory of God. Being justified freely by His grace through the redemption that is in Christ Jesus: whom God hath set forth to be a propitiation through faith in His blood, to declare His righteousness for the remission of sins that are past, through the forbearance of God. To declare, I say, at this time His righteousness. That He might be just, and the justifier of him which believeth in Jesus. Romans 3: 23-26

4. He who gave His Son to die that we might live an eternity in His presence is FOR us.

   Never does He withhold from us His best. Even in our sufferings, He is bringing us to His best, by allowing us to discover He is the treasure, love, and hope our heart desires. He will never leave us clinging to counterfeit joys that cannot satisfy.

   What shall we then say to these things? If God be for us, who can be against us? He that spared not His own Son, but delivered Him up for us all, how shall He not with Him also freely give us all things? Romans 8:31-32

   It may not be the all things you think you want. However, it will be the all things that guide you into a place of true joy-abiding and steadfast as only can be found in Him. God knows exactly what your heart needs to be able to experience His Love, His Joy, His Peace and His Glory in your life.

The Cry of Rejection

The sound of their words

What they had said

Repeatedly playing sad tunes in my head

The Scars from my past

The sorrows, regret

Like sirens whose blaring I could not forget

In darkness, alone

My heart's cry does long

To desperately feel somewhere I belong

To know I am loved

To make my appeal

Rejection the thought that seemed all too real

It wasn't their fault

How could they have known?

The scars I hid deep and never had shown

The secrets of heart

That longed to be found

That they might be healed by love to abound

The counterfeit lies

Were just a mistake

Like shattering glass my heart then to break

Oh, where is the truth

In a Dark, broken world

Where sorrows and pain are relentlessly hurled

The sin of man's pride

Has taken its toll

Wreaking havoc on each and every dear soul

Yet, if truth be told

Beneath all our will

Is a void only God's love could refill!

His Love reached beyond

The abyss we had crossed

He never considered it too great a cost

To accept rejection

Of man toward His Son

Who in His despair our victory was won!

Unworthy though I

He loved me the same

And called me as His by my very name

To be loved as His child

He is all that I need

In Him to be known and truly be freed

Freed from desires

Of counterfeit things

From trinkets and toys or frivolous flings

Grounded, secured

In God's loving arms

Freed from the lure of all this world's charms

As He draws me near

To sit for a while

Enwrapped with His joy, I truly can smile

My worries all fade

As in Him I belong

My heart can now sing a joyous love song

Chapter 3: Feelings of Guilt

Feelings of guilt can be a catalyst to transform our hearts or it can become a despair which traps us in a dark abyss of depression. For mom in her bipolar world, feelings of guilt drove her to the place of attempting suicide. She wanted to escape from her own feelings of guilt, which caused her so much pain. Never fully recognizing the depth of forgiveness from God, she was tortured by sins of the past and by the voices in her head. She knew that she was saved and that her eternal home would be with God. Trusting in the finished work of Jesus Christ on the cross, she wanted to go home to be in His presence where the pains and torments of this world no longer existed.

We cannot negate our sin, for it is real. However, our guilt must be laid before the cross of Christ alongside our sin. We can never gain victory over the sin while remaining so preoccupied with self that we cannot allow God to be the only strength to overcome it. As Ravi Zacharias wrote in his book *Cries of the Heart.*

> *When expelled by irreverence, guilt makes life in mutual harmony unlivable. When smothered by pride it makes one's life unaccountable. When concealed by fear it makes the pain unbearable. When dismissed as cultural it makes morality untenable. When claiming absolute innocence before God it makes the claim unjustifiable. When guilt surrenders to the grace of God, it makes the sin forgivable.* [5]

Haunted by Guilt

Haunted as well by guilt, I too, had a lot to learn before I could understand the joy of God in my life. Guilt often drove me back into the sin which I so desired to overcome; because, I falsely believed I must overcome it myself before God's grace could cover it. Only through

---

[5] Ravi Zacharias, *Cries of the Heart,* (Nashville, TN: W Publishing Group, 2002), 116.

learning to abide in Christ, letting go of self and pride can I or you be freed from the devastating feelings of guilt. Did I just say wallowing in our guilt is an act of pride? Yes, my own inability to accept His forgiveness is Pride and Pride is sin. I must acknowledge my inability to live a righteous Christian life before a Holy God, before, I can learn to abide in Him.

Sometimes my feelings of guilt are real, due to sin in my life that needs to be addressed. And sometimes, my feelings of guilt come from a preoccupation or belief that I am responsible for another's feelings. Much of my life, I lived with a cloud of guilt, believing that Mom's depression was my fault. Certainly, this at times lead to my responding poorly to her which added to my guilt. My responses were wrong and needed to be dealt with seeking forgiveness from God and Mom; however, the root of my guilt was based on a false premise.

What Then of Guilt?

We are all guilty of sin and unworthy of God's Grace. Feelings of guilt over our sin brings us to the cross of Jesus Christ, where all our sin and guilt was paid for. We must learn to accept our guilt before God, come to Him with a truly broken and contrite heart, and then, accept the forgiveness He has so graciously provided.

Sin scorches us most after we receive the grace of forgiveness, not before. The forgiven one realizes the gravity of the sin more when he or she is genuinely repentant and has been forgiven. God beckons our crying hearts to come to Him in repentance. This makes our sin forgiveable.[6]

Then, the sweetness of that forgiveness, the joy of knowing God's Grace, drives us daily into His presence; because, we love Him who loved us first. There we learn to abide in Him. Only He has the power to overcome sin in our

---

[6] Zacharias, *Cries,* 116

lives. We cannot ourselves. There is a freedom in letting go, dying to self-daily, forgetting our past, and allowing His power to live and shine through us.

Brethern, I count not myself to have apprehended: but this one thing I do, forgetting those things which are behind, and reaching forth unto those things which are before, I press toward the mark for the prize of the high calling of God in Christ Jesus. Philippians 3:13-14

Justification, Guilt, And the Road to Victory

Often that which drives a Christian into depression are the feelings of guilt. We see the world through our own eyes of unworthiness toward God. This can lead us to sin, rather than to allow us to rejoice in our position in Christ Jesus. When I do not fully grasp the truth that in Christ Jesus I am declared righteous by the blood of Christ which cloaks me, I become guilty of unbelief. That leads to my seeing every trial as a punishment from God, rather than seeing it as His transformative acts of Grace that build my faith.

As D Martyn Lloyd-Jones points out:

Let us remember that our justification means not only that our sins are forgiven and that we have been declared to be righteous by God Himself, not merely that we were righteous at that moment when we believed, but permanently righteous. For justification means this also, that we are given by God the positive righteousness of His own Son, the Lord Jesus Christ. That is what justification means. It does not only mean that your sins are forgiven, but much more. It means that He clothes us also with the righteousness of Jesus Christ. He says in effect: "You are righteous; I see, not a sinner, but a righteous child of My own; I see you in Christ covered by His holiness and righteousness".

And when God does that to us, He does it once and for ever. You are hidden, you yourself and your whole personality and life stand in the righteousness of Christ before

God. I say therefore, with reverence and on the authority of the Word of God that God sees your sins no more; He sees the righteousness of Christ upon you. Lay hold of that. [7]

Romans 3: 20-27

Therefore, by the deeds of the law there shall no flesh be justified in His sight: for by the law is the knowledge of sin. But now the righteousness of God without the law is manifested, being witnessed by the law and the prophets; Even the righteousness of God which is by faith of Jesus Christ unto all and upon all them that believe: for there is no difference: For all have sinned, and come short of the glory of God; Being justified freely by His grace through the redemption that is in Christ Jesus: Whom God hath set forth

---

[7] D. Martyn Lloyd-Jones, *Spiritual Depression It's Causes and Cure,* (Grand Rapids, MI: Wm. B. Eerdman Publishing, 1965), 74.

to be a propitiation through faith in His blood, to declare His righteousness for the remission of sins that are past, through the forbearance of God; To declare, I say, at this time His righteousness: that He might be just, and the justifier of Him which believeth in Jesus. Where is boasting then? It is excluded. By what law? Of works? Nay: but by the law of faith. Therefore, we concluded that a man is justified by faith without the deeds of the law.

When we, through faith, accept Jesus Christ as our Savior, our sins (past, present and future) are all forgiven. For Christ died once, bearing all of our sins declaring "It is finished" (John 19:30). Not only is our redemption complete; but, also our justification before God.

Chained by Guilt

When we become chained by guilt, we cannot see our road to victory over sin. For Mom this has been a huge issue.

She is tormented by guilt. Perhaps a word misspoken, a deed, or an overwhelming cloud at times; she finds it difficult to rest in the truth of Grace. Chained by guilt, one cannot find joy in God's road to Victory.

However, there are times when guilt can be a blessing. Just as the law was meant to open our eyes to see the vast divide between God's perfect Holiness and our sin, guilt can be just that: an opening of our eyes to see that we have allowed a separation between our self and God. We have taken our eyes off of Him and allowed sin to take reign in our lives. This is a blessing so we might come to the throne of grace, seek forgiveness and refocus our eyes upon Him our Savior. However, once our sin is recognized and laid before His throne of grace with a broken and contrite heart, we can confidently walk away knowing we have been forgiven. Not because of our own righteousness can we boldly walk away; but, rather because of His faithfulness.

Just as God reminded the children of Israel, His blessings did not come to them because of their righteousness. Instead it came because of His Covenant Love and faithfulness. He chose to deal with them by Mercy.

Neither do I suggest that we consider our sin, flippantly. To do that means that we really do not understand the gift of grace we have been given or the cost Christ paid for our forgiveness.

Focusing on Guilt is Sin

When we are consumed by guilt for sins past, we are guilty of the sin of disbelief. In effect, we are saying that God has not done what He promised. That is, God has not forgiven us fully as He said He would do. He knows that we are frail, earthen vessels incapable of living a righteous life apart from His power within us. (2 Corinthians 4:7). Yet, if I remain focused on my past sins, even then, I have taken my eyes off Him and have focused my eyes once more on me.

Certainly, that will lead to more failures; because when I am focused on me, I am not focused upon Him.

Only when I take my eyes off of me, focus on His Victory at the cross, can I hope to sin less. It is His power within me which holds firm the victory over sin. To do that I must keep my heart and mind focused on Him, through reading His Word, learning of Him, and falling in love with Him fresh each morning.

A Seared Conscience Free of Guilt?

While we are not to be chained by the guilt of our past, we must not become complacent or tolerant of our sin. We stand justified before God, because of the blood of Christ which covers our sin. Yet, we cannot; therefore, "sin that grace might abound" (Romans 6:1-2). The sudden pangs of guilt when we sin serves to bring us to our knees and the Word of God. We are in the process of being transformed into the image of Christ. "The Lord will perfect that which concerneth me" (Psalm 138:8). The process at times is a searing fire. He is always about the work of transforming each believer into the righteous image of Christ which He has declared us to be. We must not mistakenly allow our conscience to be seared.

When God created mankind, He gave them a conscience, a moral compass. Even the nonbeliever has a compass between good and bad, a law within their own hearts. This compass provides further proof of the existence of God. Evolution alone cannot provide a moral compass, since survival of the fittest would never consider morality a goal. Indeed, murder, lies, self-promotion whatever the cost to another would all be considered good, if survival were the only goal. As Paul wrote, there is a law written on our conscience given by God.

"For when the Gentiles, which have not the law, do by nature the things contained in the law, these, having not the

law, are a law unto themselves: Which shew the work of the law written in their heart, their conscience also bearing witness, and their thoughts the mean while accusing or else excusing one another" Romans 2:14-15.

Justification Does Not Mean a Seared Conscience

It is true that the believer stands justified before God, his or hers sins all covered by the blood of Christ. That truth means that we are not to be chained by sins of our past. However, it does not mean that our conscience is to be seared so that we no longer feel the pangs of guilt for present sins. Distinguishing between good and evil in our daily life is necessary. We have not yet become fully what we shall be.

That God does not account our sin against us anymore, does not mean our sin is unaccountable. It means that our salvation is secure. However, our ability to know the joy of our relationship with Him is affected. As David in his prayer of repentance pleaded, "Restore unto me the joy of my salvation" (Psalms 51:12). Ah, but look at why he believed this so important, "Then will I teach transgressors thy ways; and sinners shall be converted unto thee" (Psalms 51:13). Shouldn't that be our goal as a Christian as well?

Our Groaning Over Sin and Our Helper

"Because the creature itself also shall be delivered from the bondage of corruption into the glorious liberty of the children of God. For we know that the whole creation groaneth and travaileth in pain together until now. And not only they, but ourselves also, which have the firstfruits of the Spirit, even we ourselves groan within ourselves, waiting for the adoption, to wit, the redemption of our body. For we are saved by hope" (Romans 8:21-24)

We are to groan whenever we fail God; but, we are not to be chained by our guilt. Our groaning with frailty is to bring us back to the foot of the cross. We are not to forget that we have been forgiven. However, forgiveness cannot mean that I take sin lightly. Christ paid for my sin. I must turn my eyes to the Savior seeing fully the price He paid for my sin while at the same time standing in the hope that one day I will look like Him. Only then, do I see the sorrowful circumstances of this life as "good." For God uses every circumstance to bring me closer to Him where He is transforming my heart to reflect the righteousness He has freely given. He has given us a helper in all of this.

"Likewise, the Spirit also helpeth our infirmities: for we know not what we should pray for as we ought: but the Spirit itself maketh intercession for us with groanings which cannot be uttered. And He that searcheth the hearts knoweth what is the mind of the Spirit, because He maketh intercession for the saints according to the will of God. And we know that all things work together for good to them that

love God, to them who are the called according to His purpose" (Romans 8:26-28).

A Seared Conscience

In this world we have seen acts of pure evil and wondered how that could be. Those are people for whom their conscience is seared. No longer do they hold a moral compass. The lies of this world have completely eradicated their ability to know right from wrong. In fact, they believe themselves always right, never feeling guilt for their actions. *"In the latter times some shall depart from the faith, giving heed to seducing spirits, and doctrines of devils; speaking lies in hypocrisy; having their conscience seared with a hot iron"* (I Timothy 4:1-2).

Unfortunately, we have come to even see this within the modern-day church. All those who deny the power of the cross. Salvation can only come through faith in Jesus Christ. We, as Christians, must not abandon the truth of the Gospel message.

Concerning My Guilt and Shame

Mom's bipolar disease lead her to waiver between feelings of self-aggrandizement and dark depressions from guilt. Within that world it is hard not to be overtaken by the highest feelings of joy, moments where she felt God intimately, followed by overwhelming sorrow when she felt she had failed Him. Then, she would feel abandoned for her own sins and failures.

Growing up surrounded by her emotional highs and lows, I, also, believed God's love and blessings were dependent upon my ability to always get things right. Every failure I feared would lead to His Anger and harsh punishment. My fears, shame and guilt would push me to "work harder" while at the same time keeping me separated from fully understanding His Grace. The harder I worked, the more I failed.

It took many years to learn that only when I rest in His love, His grace, abiding in Christ's finished work on the cross, could I hope to live this Christian life. I cannot overcome sin in my life without His strength. He already won the victory for my sin. Until my heart recognized that before Him, I stand clothed in the righteousness of Christ; I lived in constant unhealthy fear before God. When I looked in the mirror I saw the filthy rags of my own unrighteousness. I cannot live in His abiding, steadfast joy unless my heart knows the truth of my position in Christ Jesus. Neither can I find victory in my day to day life unless I, by faith, trust in His victory. But God did not want to leave me there. His love was so great that His plan was to teach me of His unconditional love and all-encompassing forgiveness. He did that through Pete.

Overcoming the Chains of Guilt and Shame

By the age of 24 I was already divorced twice. Overwhelmed by guilt and shame, I believed that God could never bless me with the greatest desire of my heart. More than anything else I wanted a husband that loved me. I wanted to please God. Yet, somehow, I believed I would know I had when He provided me with someone who truly loved me. That would be the proof that God was pleased with me. He would fulfill this desire of my heart and send someone who would love me with all their heart. Then, I met Pete. Pete was very handsome with a brilliant mind. I felt so unworthy of him; yet, he asked me to marry him. Over the years, I came to realize that he was bipolar, much like Mom. Although, his bipolar came with moments of violence, whereas hers came with moments of psychosis. As I would to quickly learn, often the violence perpetrated by someone suffering from bipolar disease is exhibited toward the ones they trust the most.

At first, I would blame myself for each act of violence. If I could only be better, work harder, or even were prettier, then he could truly love me. Oddly, that was much the way I looked at God. God could only truly love me if I were able to be better, work harder and stand firmer in my faith, on my own strength.

Oddly enough, it was through the difficulties in my marriage, that I came to understand God's unconditional love and forgiveness. It was through the pain and difficulties I found the truth of God's love as well.

Once, I began to realize Pete's frailties and illness; born from a life of pain himself, I no longer was a victim. Yet, I chose to stay because I loved Him. God always softened my heart to see Pete through His eyes. I could see the good and beauty deep within his heart. Furthermore, I saw his pain and wanted so much to heal the shattered pieces of his heart. Unconditional love and forgiveness over shadowed any and every offense. Somewhere amid it all, I came to realize my human heart held not the capacity for this and this was God in me that forgave and loved Pete this way. Then, the epiphany. If God could cause my human heart to love this way, how much greater was God's love for me.

God's Bigger Plan of Glory

But God's plans were much bigger than just me. He also shone forth Himself to Pete, through the holes of my heart. He wooed Pete to accept Christ as His Lord and Savior before Pete's death, thereby transforming his eternity. Through it all, God opened my eyes to see the truth of His love, transformed Pete's eternity, and ultimately led Mom to a place of peace and joy. Pete is now in heaven in God's presence, no longer suffering the pains of this world. Mom is happy for the first time in her life. Although, that truth came many years and many lessons later. But what a blessing! Now, I witness Mom experiencing joy and peace.

We had many more roads to travel together along this journey. I had more cobwebs and chaff to be removed from my heart. Yet, I was on my way to discovering a life resting in God's love. God was writing the wondrous truth of the gospel on my heart that I might also share it with you.

7 Lessons from God Concerning My Guilt and Shame

1. Because Jesus Christ bore all my sin, my guilt, and my shame upon the cross; I, by faith, am free from it's penalty. Furthermore, I stand before God justified, cloaked in the righteousness of Christ. No longer am I to be chained by guilt or shame for sins of my past.

2. God's love for me is unconditional and His forgiveness all encompassing. Nothing can separate me from that love; because, of the blood of Christ shed for me.

3. Every detail of my life is in His Mighty Hands of love. He takes all the broken pieces and transforms them into the likeness of His Precious Son. One step at a time, He is transforming my heart from the inside out.

4. I cannot transform another's heart, only God can. My place is to pray for them, pray for wisdom; then, to proclaim the truth of the gospel message through my life and my words. God does the rest.

5. When guilt comes, I need to discern if this is merely conviction for a sin I need to confess or is it's Satan whispering words to cause me to stumble. To know the difference, I must be diligently studying His word and seeking Him in prayer.

6. God is my greatest treasure. In Him is found abiding, steadfast joy.

7. The more I know Him, the more I love Him.

Guilty I AM

Guilty I Am and guilty I'd be

Now and forever, eternally

Were it not for Christ at Calvary

Who paid my price, to set me free!

Oh, precious Grace help me to see

Reflections of you inside that be

Born from a heart of humility

Help me to come to the end of me

That Your Love is all that the world can see

Chapter 4:

Jealousy: Like Flames from Hell!

Certainly, jealousy should never play a role in my relationship with Mom, that would be ludicrous! I knew that! Even more so, after I found out she suffered so from bipolar disease. Perhaps that is why I blew it off or worse, I stuffed it deep inside me where jealousy could grow like the flames of Hell burning within a dark crevice of my heart where I forbid anyone to see. If I never uttered the words or gave credence to its existence; then, maybe it would go away. Yet, God knew it was there and that it would have to dealt with. He knew that for His true love to reign in my heart, the chaff of jealousy had to be done away with, once and for all. Because if truth be known, who was the rage of my jealousy really against, if not God, Himself.

When the Shulamite woman looked off into the distance, she saw someone on the arms of her beloved and cried out; "Set me as a seal upon your heart, as a seal upon your arm; for love is as strong as death, Jealousy as cruel as the grave. Its flames are flames of fire, a most vehement flame" (Song of Solomon 8:6 NKJV).

As I begin to explain the jealousy I felt, you might say, "How foolish!" Yet, stop for a moment, look deep within your own heart to see if any jealousy is lurking there. It was certainly there in the hearts of the apostles. I want to begin with dissecting the various forms of jealousy one might face and then tell you more specifically about mine and how God dealt with it.

Jealousy in the Hearts of the Apostles

We cannot help but notice in the account of the rich young ruler, how quickly Peter responded, "See, we have left all and followed you. Therefore, what shall we have?" (Matthew 19:27 NKJV). The seed of jealousy begins there. "Lord, what will you give me for **MY** faithfulness." Have we so quickly forgotten He called us and He opened our eyes that we might desire to follow Him? Isn't His presence enough?

While working in the jail ministry, I noticed some who would profess salvation just because they wanted God to rescue them and suddenly make their life easy. It wasn't about true repentance or love toward God. Instead, it was a get out of jail free card they wanted. They did not want God, only His gifts. We see that within our churches and society as well, all too often. The question I came to ask them was: "If God never gave you what you asked for. If heaven and hell were not on the line. Would you love God for who He is in all His Glory and desire to be in His presence? Would He be your greatest desire?" When their answer was "No!" Then, I said, "I fear you do not know Him at all."

Beyond, "what will you give me for following you"; we find that the apostles often murmured amongst themselves as to who was the greater and would hold the greatest position in

Christ's Kingdom one day. You can see that in Mark 10:35-47, Matthew 20:20-21, and Luke 22:24.

Furthermore, when Christ foretold of Peter's cruel death, Peter's first response was: "What about him? As he pointed to John" (John 21:21). Jesus replied, "what is that to you, follow me" (John 21:22).

The apostles' actions and thoughts were very much like our own, if we are honest. We want to compare God's love toward us with His love for another. We want to be first. Why God is he or she a success and I am struggling? Don't you love me? Thusly, jealousy turns the truth of Grace and God's goodness into doubts and questions which eat at the spirit. So, we must address these feelings at their roots before we can know the peace which in Christ Jesus is freely ours. Peace is a gift from God that we may often fail to claim.

Confronting Jealousy Head On.

Over the next few pages, together we will explore jealousy. As we do so, I bid you open your heart and ask God to reveal to you if lurking there are some dusty shreds of jealousy or envy. Only when we recognize its presence can we honesty bring its filthy rags to the cross of Christ. If not, it will grow into a raging fire from the pits of hell to destroy our testimony and to keep us chained to anger, guilt and depression. Jesus Christ died on the cross to release us from the chains of sin. Before God, through faith, every believer stands justified adorned by the righteousness of Christ.

However, when we adorn those filthy rags of jealousy before the world, they cannot see Jesus Christ's righteousness shining through us. Satan cannot steal our salvation; but, he can certainly try to mess up our witness for Christ. God will transform our hearts, one step at a time. For me, I had to first recognize and name my jealousy; then, lay it at the foot of the cross. Only then could I be freed from its chains, so I could truly experience the abiding, steadfast joy I had been given in Christ Jesus.

The Utter Insanity of My Jealous Thoughts

Both Mom and Pete found it difficult to demonstrate love. Within their bipolar minds, there lay a fear of vulnerability. Therefore, any action of love would soon be followed by a harsh rebuke or criticism of the one they loved. Living in that world of criticism, I spent a lifetime in search of love. Desperate to find love, only to discover it had been there with me all along. God's love had been there expectantly waiting for me from eternity past. It was His love that had brought me to Him that day I accepted Christ as my Savior. And it was His love that indwelled me, guiding every step so that I might come to know His fullness of joy. Along this journey, His precious hands were guiding me every step of the way. So, I even understood the utter insanity of my jealous thoughts, which is probably why I neatly tried to hide them.

Yet, just as you cannot get rid of a cancer by ignoring it, neither can you get rid of jealous thoughts by pretending their nonexistence. The only way to deal with cancer is to biopsy it, name it, and then attack it aggressively. Jealous thoughts must be confronted with the same aggressiveness as one would attack a cancer. Because Jealous thoughts when ignored will grow to consume you with anger. Which in turn, will cause you to take yours eyes off Jesus and cause you to place impenetrable walls around your heart. Hoping God would not notice the jealousy and anger, you withdraw into your own spiraling insanity of guilt, shame and depression. While at the same time, putting on an outward show of self-righteous behavior and righteous indignation. Placing all the blame on the object of your jealous thoughts.

Dissecting My Jealous Thoughts

When I finally had to dissect my jealous thoughts toward Mom, I discovered there were two major forms.

1. Mom had someone to take care of her. She did not have to take responsibility for herself; because, there was Daddy and then, now there was me. On the other hand, I had to march forward through every storm making all the tough decisions, facing the consequences of my own poor decisions at times, and bear the weight of the world, alone! (Ok, not very logical, utter insanity of thought, and certainly not bearing even a resemblance of the truth of the gospel). Which is why I wanted to bury it instead of facing it head on. Satan loves to attack us this way, so we don't just grab the "sword of the Spirit, which is the word of God" (Ephesians 6:17) to squelch Satan's effects on our hearts and minds.

2. There were times while Mom lived with me that I had to hire people to come into the home to care for her. This was financially a severe strain at times; but, she needed the help because of lapses in judgement, deep bouts of depression, and even psychotic moments. Then, when mom became obsessed with talking about how wonderful the person caring for her was, I would feel hurt, overwhelmed with jealous thoughts, and angry. Instead of rejoicing that she was happy, I became bitter. Again, I realize the utter insanity of my feelings. Yet, jealousy is like that. However, unless I acknowledged my feeling and then conquered them in my own heart with the truth of the gospel I could not gain victory over them. Instead they kept growing like a cancer until the flames burned like the flames from hell in my own heart.

The Utter Insanity of it ALL

As I pointed out, I could not overcome jealous thoughts until I first of all called them out, named them, dissected them and then laid them at the foot of the cross. If you look at both examples of my utter insanity of thought, they both go back to much the same human thoughts of the apostles. "What will You give me God for following you and being faithful?" And, "Lord, do you love me more than her or him?" Both of these come from the sin of pride and self-exaltation, as do nearly all sin begin. To overcome this, I needed God's Holy Spirit to reveal the darkness of this ugly blemish in my heart and remind me of the whole truth of the gospel.

God loved me with the same intensity as He did Mom and He loved Mom with the same intensity as He did me. There was no difference in His Grace nor His Love. "God is no respecter of persons" (Acts 10:34; Romans 2:11). He who formed my innermost being (Psalm 139:13) and knew me before I was ever born (Jeremiah 1:5) had designed the perfect plan for my life. Every detail, even the sorrows, struggles and pains were precisely designed for me. He knew exactly what would be needed to draw me into His bosom where I would find His abiding, steadfast joy. Furthermore, He knew the same for mom. Beyond that, He knew what was needed to bring Pete to a saving knowledge of Him.

Oh, to Be Perfected in Love

Secondly, when I was more concerned with Mom seeing the sacrificial love I was showing through providing her with people to care for her; then, I was not truly loving her. I wanted the glory, meaning I was selfish in my desires that her happiness be only found in me. Perfect love would be more concerned with her joy than her response to me. My sacrificial love had become selfish love instead. God wants to perfect us in love. Sometimes, that means we need God's painful surgeon's scalpel to cut out the cancer of selfishness; that, we might be filled to the overflowing with His perfect love.

This is what Jesus prayed for us in John 17: 23 "I in them, and thou in me, that they may be made perfect in one; and that the world may know that thou hast sent me, and hast loved them, as thou has loved me." If I truly know that God loves me with the same depth of love He has for Jesus Christ, His perfect Holy Son; then, why would I ever try to compare His love to another here on earth.

And we have known and believed the love that God hath to us. God is love: and he that dwelleth in love dwelleth in God, and God in him. Herein is OUR LOVE MADE PERFECT, that we may have boldness in the day of judgment: because as He is, so are we in this world. There is no fear in love; but PERFECT LOVE casteth out fear.

Because fear hath torment. He that feareth is not made perfect in love. I John 4: 16-18

If God Is A Jealous God, Why Is Jealousy Bad?

In the book of Exodus, we find that the children of Israel became impatient and fearful. Moses had gone high into the mountain to meet with God. They could only see the fire surrounding the mountain. Despite all that God had done to guide and protect them, they became restless while waiting. Then, they decided to build a golden calf to worship. They sang and danced in worship to this golden image of their own making. God commanded Moses to descend and deal with the people. When he did, in anger Moses broke the tablets of the law. Once he had destroyed the golden calf and rebuked the people, he pleaded to God for the people. God forgave them. Moses ascended the mountain with new tablets.

God said, "thou shalt worship no other god: for the Lord, whose name is Jealous, is a jealous God" Exodus 34:14.

So, how are we to interpret this? If God is a jealous god, then is jealousy bad? How is His jealousy different than ours? To help us understand this, we need to first of all look to the preceding verses.

A Righteous and Jealous God?

And the Lord descended in the cloud, and stood with him there, and proclaimed the name of the Lord. And the Lord passed by before him, and proclaimed, "The Lord, The Lord God, merciful and gracious, longsuffering, and abundant in goodness and truth, keeping mercy for thousands, forgiving iniquity and transgression and sin, and that will by no means clear the guilty. ...Behold I make a covenant: before all thy people I will do marvels, such as have not been done in all the earth, nor in any nation: and all the people among which thou art shall see the work of the Lord" (Exodus 34:5-7,10).

God's jealousy toward His people, is not one built out of fear or envy. He is a jealous God; because, He loves us and as our Creator knows our hearts can never be fully satisfied apart from Him. All these other counterfeit joys we seek or think will satisfy, only lead to brokenness. This is quite different from the jealousy that you or I have toward others. Ours is either built on envy or is more concerned about our feelings than it is about the other. Look at these lyrics from *Jealous* by Labyrinth.

'Cause I wished you the best of

All this world could give

And I told you when you left me

There's nothing to forgive

But I always thought you'd come back,

Tell me all you found was

Heartbreak and misery

It's hard for me to say,

I'm jealous of the way

You're happy without me.[8]

Our hearts don't really want them to be happy, we just say that. Indeed, we are envious of their happiness without us. On the other hand, God is not envious of our happiness. Instead, He desires our happiness. However, He also knows that He is the only true source of our happiness. Therefore, His jealousy is one born out of His love for us, recognizing that our hearts will only be broken by the idols we build and the counterfeit joys that we desire.

Defining Jealousy

If you look up the definition of jealousy, the first two definitions deal with envy. Yet, if you look at the root of the

[8] Labyrinth, *Jealous*, *https://www.google.com/search?q=lyrics+to+jealous+by+labrinth&oq =lyrics+to+jealous&aqs=chrome.1.69i57j0l5.13780j1j7&sourceid=chro me&ie=UTF-8* Accessed 7/11/18

word you will find that it came from the medieval Latin word zelosus which became zealous and then later jealous. For that reason, if you look at the third definition of jealous, you will find it to be "fiercely protective or vigilant of one's rights or possessions."[9]

God wants to protect us from the heartbreaks of this world and He knows that true joy, peace, hope and love are found in Him alone. His jealousy, unlike ours, is based on His Mercy, Grace, and Love for us. All that He does in our life has one purpose: our joy. That abiding, steadfast joy can only be found in Him. When we recognize that truth, everything changes. Even our trials have meaning when we see them through His eyes of Love, Grace, and Mercy.

God is passionately, devoted and committed to bringing you close to His heart. His covenant of love to all who accept Jesus Christ as their Savior is to write His "laws

---

[9] https://www.google.com/search?q=Dictionary#dobs=jealous Accessed 7/11/18.

into their hearts, and in their minds...And their sins and iniquities will (He) remember no more" (Hebrews 10:16).

So, my one question to you is? Do you know Jesus Christ as your Lord and Savior? Without the blood of Christ, there is no remission for sin. Have you been washed in the blood? There is no other name under heaven by which men might be saved. (Acts 4:12).

So, What About My Jealous Rage?

The longer I stuffed those insane feelings of jealousy toward Mom into a box within my heart, the larger the flames grew. I tried to tell myself I only wanted her best. After all, sooner or later those whom I paid to care for her would all be gone. Only I would be standing, fighting for her. I desperately wanted her to see that and to just love me. Didn't she see the sacrifices I was making? I tried to proclaim my sacrifice as love for her. However, the lies I told my heart did not make the jealousy go away. Instead they fanned the flames into a jealous rage, burning within me. I could not see, that my love was not really love if I was more concerned about me than her. My sacrifice was not born out of love; rather, it was a vain attempt at self-exaltation.

Peter's Lesson on Pride

Sometimes along this journey of life, God allows us to move forward falling head first into the mud. He allows us to fail so that we might lay aside the pride and look honestly at the rubbish within our own hearts. To cleanse us, purify us and transform our hearts into the image of Christ, He first must open our eyes to see the truth. We must see the blemishes before we are willing to seek His cleansing. Much like Peter when Christ foretold of his denying Him.

Remember what Jesus said, "Simon, Simon, behold, Satan hath desired to have you, that he may sift you as wheat" (Luke 22:31). Satan wanted to destroy Peter's faith-to rip it from him. But Jesus prayed for Peter, that his faith would not fail him. What a wondrous thought! When Satan tries to steal my faith or destroy my testimony, Jesus is praying for me.

(Hebrews 7:25, Romans 8:34). Satan could not destroy or sift away Peter's faith. Instead, God allowed Satan's sifting, knowing that He (God) would use that to sift away Peter's pride. What a blow that must have been to Satan! He could no longer use Peter's pride to destroy his testimony. What Satan meant for evil, God used for good.

Jealousy Born Out of Fear

One more point regarding jealousy that we must address is that jealously is born out of fear. We fear that we may lose someone or something. Or, we may fear that we will be facing pain, sorrow or loss of another kind. Pride and fear live close at hand. Because, we recognize that our pride is unmerited. Although we try to make the world think we are great, deep within we must realize we are broken. Living in constant fear that the truth be known, we cling to pride which gives birth to jealousy.

So, what were the lessons God taught me to overcome my jealous rage

5 Lessons from God Regarding Jealousy

1. Be Honest and Open Regarding Yourself

   I was so ashamed to admit my jealous rage to myself and even more so, to God. My own pride or need to feel righteous caused me to hide the truth of my feelings from me. That never works! At some point, all the flames of jealous rage would emerge; spewing forth like volcanic lava and destroying life. "If we say that we have no sin, we deceive ourselves, and the truth is not in us. If we confess our sins, He is faithful and just to forgive us our sins and to cleanse us from all unrighteousness" (I John 1:8-9). Before I could confess my sin of jealous rage, I had to see it and name it. For jealous rage is a sin against God, first and foremost.

2. Recognize My Utter Helplessness Against It

   As long as I try to fix it with my own strength, I fail. I do not have the strength to overcome my own frailties. Only God can do that. The sooner I recognize that fact, the sooner I can humbly confess my sin and allow God to cleanse my heart of the evils of jealous rage. Remember when Jesus spoke of the rich, young ruler who left sad because he did not want to leave his riches? The apostles asked Jesus, "Who can be saved?" His reply was, "With men this is impossible; but, with God all things are possible" (Matthew 19:26).

3. Acknowledge That Jealous Rage Is Against God

Our feelings of jealous rage are actually an act against God. It is saying to God, I am dissatisfied with what you have chosen for me. The Bible speaks of this often as envy. Where ever envy lies, faith dies. As I have often quoted Hebrews 11:6, "Faith is knowing God IS and He is the rewarder of them who diligently seek Him." If I truly believe God is Sovereign and that He rewards those who diligently seek Him, then, I will rejoice in all that He sends into my life. Knowing He only sends me His best. As we read in Proverbs 14:30, "A sound heart is the life of the flesh: buy envy the rottenness of the bones." A sound heart is one who trusts God, abiding in His Sovereign Grace.

Or look at James 3:16: "For where envying and strife is, there is confusion and every evil work." Acknowledge the truth, jealous rage toward another is sin against God and cannot be eradicated until you confess it as such. Then ask God to help your faith to grow. This may mean He will give you more trials and tribulations to face while growing your faith, but it is definitely well worth the pain and sorrow. As grows your faith, so grows your joy and satisfaction in all that He has given you. Jealousy will disappear as your faith enlarges.

4. Perfecting Us in Love

God redeems all who accept Jesus Christ as their Savior. Additionally, God justifies the believer, declaring them as righteous because He has cloaked each of us with the righteousness of Christ. While in this journey on earth, He is ever about the task of transforming us into the image of Jesus

Christ. Furthermore, He is perfecting us in love. That means, as He is writing His words upon our hearts, He is chipping away at our hearts of stone. In order for us to love as He loved, the fragments of our selfish, self-exalting human nature must be broken down and swept away. Yet, God does this with such patience, lovingly knowing that as we are perfected in His love our joy will become overflowing. Peace, hope, love, and faith will remain.

I Corinthians 13:4-8 (NKJV) *Love suffers long and is kind. love does not envy. Love does not parade itself, is not puffed up; does not behave rudely, does not seek its own, is not provoked, thinks no evil; does not rejoice in iniquity, but rejoices in the truth; bears all things, believes all things, hopes all things, endures all things. Love never fails.*

5. Learn from Jesus

As noted, we cannot transform our own hearts. But, God can. What we can do is to confess our sin, lay it at the foot of the cross. Spend time in prayer. Ask God to grow our faith; particularly, because, jealousy makes it obvious ours is faltering. Jesus said; "Take my yoke upon you and learn of me; for I am meek and lowly in heart: and ye shall find rest unto your souls" (Matthew 11:29). If you have ever felt jealous rage, you know there is no rest for your soul there.

Soren Kierkegaard wrote concerning this kind of meekness as follows. "So, meekness bears the heavy burden lightly, and the burden of a wrong inflicted, so lightly that it seems as if the offence of the guilty one were lessened."[10]

Meekness would mean I would have born even that which I believed were offenses or wrongs inflicted unwittingly by Mom. It could never have developed into the jealous rage that I felt. Thank God, He in His grace did not give up on me. Rather He ever so gently opened my eyes to see the truth.

---

[10] Kierkegaard, *Sufferings*, 43-44

Fear Walked In

Fear walked in

I let her stay

And Talk with me a while

What harm was she

A lonely soul

She could not mean me guile

But as she talked

With gentle voice

I listened to her tale

It seemed to touch

A chord in me

My heart began to wale

Jealousy

She was her friend

Who also came to stay.

A little while

What could it harm?

As hours turned to days

Another friend
Came close behind
And anger was her name
I could not hear
The voice of God
While playing their wild games

I bid them leave
Get out of here
I screamed at them to go
I let them in
My fault I know
Oh, such a wretched foe

I cried to God
To make them leave
I want to feel your love
I need your joy
Your grandest peace
My eyes to see above

He heard my plea

He bade them leave

My faith He did restore

I felt His love

His warm embrace

How could I want for more?

I looked around

And then I saw

A precious love was gone

I'd lost him there

Oh, wretched self

I knew I'd done such wrong.

So, if you see

That one called fear

Come knocking at your door

Don't let her in

Bolt tight the locks

Or run to distant shores

Hold tight to God

His truth, His love

And never doubt His word

For fear will bring

Along her friends

Your loss, your fault, Absurd.

A Jealous Thread Had Filled My Heart

A jealous thread had filled my heart
That from God's truth I did depart
So, blinded by my thoughts of me
His love no longer could I see

Forgotten was the truth of grace
No longer could I see His face
Nor understand His plan for me
Was forged by Him to set me free

Desiring then His plan for her
His love for me became a blur
How could He love her more than me?
While sorrow then became my plea

His patient, gentle love then held
Unto my heart, though I rebelled
The flames of anger rose in me
Only His truth could set me free

Twas there He reached into my heart
To wash my sin, His love impart
His plan designed was best for me
Wrought from His love eternally

The trials that my life had faced
Had brought me low, til I embraced
Him as the only hope for me
The only treasure I could see

His love and grace there did abound
And overflow with joyous sound
His glory reaching forth to me
And point me to that rugged tree

On which He died that I might be
His precious love eternally
He'd planned the perfect life for me
That I might love with purity

He broke the chains that held me tight
The jealous threads that bound my night
Then filled me with His Love for me
Opened my eyes His heart to see

Amazing Grace! My Sovereign King
Had filled my heart with joy to sing
His plan had been His best for me
To learn to love with purity

Chapter 5:

Where is God in Our Suffering?

Within the previous chapters, I addressed my own responses to Mom. Reactions of shame, guilt, and jealousy. Also, I began telling you of God's lessons of life through each phase. Furthermore, I spoke of how God used my marriage to Pete to learn of God's unconditional love toward me by allowing my heart to experience unconditional love and forgiveness toward Pete. But what of Mom and Pete? What were the emotions that they suffered? How could it be that God allowed their suffering? Could their suffering have divine purpose? Such agonizing suffering within their minds would seem so useless unless you see even that through the eyes of a loving God! Only time allowed me to see their suffering. Wrought with guilt over their own actions, they demonstrated often a forgiveness toward me unparalleled to my lack of forgiveness. At times, like a lion caged, I lashed out with words that cut deep. My anger and response, I felt were justified at the time; but, alas, they were not.

My journey, as well as theirs, through dark and winding paths of suffering were all guided by God's Hand of love. My angry response to perceived wrongs, in truth were born out of a lack of faith or obedience to God. Though I may at times have believed, my anger, sorrow, and unrest were born out of a righteous indignation for their wrongs. The truth is: God is Sovereign. My suffering, as was theirs, came from an Almighty, Sovereign God who always remains more concerned with our eternity than our momentary comfort. Yet, in the midst of all that suffering, He bids us to draw closer to Him. There, abiding in His arms of Grace, we learn to lay aside all else that we might find true Joy, Peace, and Rest in Him. For He truly is the treasure that our weary hearts seek to find.

TRUE JOY FOUND IN SUFFERING?

Our journey here is preparing us for an eternity of joy in His presence, surrendered to and surrounded by His Perfect Love. Beyond that, He bids us to discover that abiding, steadfast joy here and now.

None of us would say as we begin this journey of following Christ that we desire suffering. Yet, we are told of Him, the perfect righteous Son of God who is Truth itself; "that He learned obedience through suffering." (Hebrews 5:8). He, who is equal to God, joint-creator of the universe, and co-designer of this plan of salvation, humbled Himself in obedience to suffering upon this earth. Not that He had ever been disobedient; rather, He learned of the very nature of submission and obedience through His suffering. He who came to die that mankind might be offered salvation free and full, suffered the mockery and ridicule of the very ones He came to save. Humbly, He submitted Himself to ridicule and the empty words of faith from even His followers. So, often, they, as we are, were more concerned about His gifts than knowing Him.

Yet, God bids us to come to Him, to abide in Him. There we may find rest for our souls and joy for our heart. However, to truly know Him, we must join in His suffering. Yet it is with such patience and tender mercy that He guides us through the suffering. In suffering, we learn to let go of the selfish desires that bind us to this world and keep us from Him.

THE SUFFERING OF CHRIST AND OBEDIENCE

Perhaps Soren Kierkegaard said it best.

"Ah! The one who knew all, whose thoughts comprehend all, who needed not to come to the knowledge of anything, because what He knows not does not even exist, of Him is it said that He learned obedience by the things which He suffered.

Christ learned obedience. Indeed, from eternity His will accorded with the Father's, and He freely chose the Father's will. But when, as in the fulness of the time, He came, thereupon he learned obedience by the things which He suffered—which He suffered when He came to His own, and they did not know Him, when He went about here in the humble guise of a servant, and bore the weight of God's eternal plan, and His words were spoken as if in vain, when He, in whom, in whom alone there is salvation, was in the world as something superfluous...when nobody heeded Him, or, what was harder when He aroused the worthless interest of a vagrant curiosity....Even the vinegar was not a drink more sour for the Holy One, than the vacuous interest taken by the idles, and the

revolting tribute curiosity accorded Him who
is the Truth!"[11]

The True Joy Set Before Us

Now, standing in the presence of God, do you think that Pete would bemoan the suffering he endured upon this earth? Nor would Mom who has finally find the joy of being in His presence here on earth through prayer and reading His word. It has been through the suffering I endured, that I have come to learn of Him. I too have learned to trust in Him and to let God be God. For it is in learning, through suffering, that His plan is best for me. "the sufferer painfully learns, first, that in spite of all, it is God who ordains, and then goes on to learn in glad obedience, to leave to God to ordain!"[12]

Wherefore seeing we also are compassed about with so great a cloud of witnesses, let us lay aside every weight, and the sin which doth so easily beset us, and let us run with

---

[11] Kierkegaard, *Sufferings, 52-53*
[12] Kierkegaard, *Sufferings, 58.*

patience the race that is set before us. Looking unto Jesus the author and finisher of our faith. Who for the joy that was set before Him endured the cross, despising the shame, and is set down at the right hand of the throne of God. For consider Him that endured such contradiction of sinners against Himself, lest ye be wearied and faint in your minds (Hebrews 12:1-3).

How can a Sovereign, Loving God Ordain Agony?

It is the question that we as Christians avoid voicing aloud. There are some great Christian scholars who enter the debate scene to defend God on this very question. I do not pretend myself to be one of them. Rather, I am a child of God, who spent a lifetime seeking an answer within my own heart and mind to that very question. How can a Sovereign, Loving God Ordain Agony, Suffering and Pain? This was a question that even as a young child, I agonized over. Whenever I watched mom and daddy fight, I shuddered in pain. Daddy would sit quiet with head in hand, as mom screamed and even threw things. The agony of my heart, wanting to comfort Daddy and not even understanding what the fight was about.

I felt agony and pain when then in grade school I watched a child be punished unjustly. At least in my eyes, unjustly. Somehow my little heart could see within another's heart to understand when they weren't rebelliously disobeying. Others I knew deserved punishment, went free.

When years later mom was diagnosed with bipolar disorder, the question echoed in my mind. If God is Sovereign and He is loving, why does mom suffer the agony of her bipolar disease? She knew Him as Savior, so why did He not just heal her?

Then, when crouched into a corner with arms covering my head while being beaten and kicked; again, I asked the question. How can a Sovereign, Loving God allow such agony in my life? Furthermore, how could He ordain me to stay with Pete? Because I clearly could hear God command me to stay. Furthermore, God opened my heart to forgive and love unconditionally through it all, something impossible for my heart to do alone.

Does God Ordain Agony, or merely Allow?

Ordain means to order. This is not the same as create. God did not create evil or sin. However, if I truly believe that God is Sovereign; then, I must believe He ordains even the painful things that come into my life. His very Holy, Righteous, Just and Loving nature exists. He is the essence of all that is good and right. Absence of Him by simple logic is absence of holiness, righteousness, justice, and love. Just as darkness does not exist, rather, it is the absence of light. Evil is the absence of God. Oh, don't get me wrong. I am not saying that the unbeliever cannot feel or know of love or justice. What I am saying is they do only because of God's common grace in the world. He displays Himself to the world through many ways and means.

As a Christian, I know that every detail of my life is ordained by God. I also know that He has promised that "all things work together for good" (Romans 8:28). Not just the pretty, nice and easy things, all things. Why would He have ordained agony, pain and sorrow in my life? Or for that matter in Mom's Life or Pete's? Was it not His wisdom that knew exactly what our hearts needed to seek Him! His desire is for our best and greatest joy. Yet, He knows that can only be found in a relationship with Him. He created us and knows we cannot find true Being apart from Him.

What I have learned over the years is that I can trust Him completely. Would I know His Heart of Love or His Abiding, Steadfast Joy the way that I do today had I not walked through agony and sorrow? I daresay no.

THE PROBLEM OF EVIL

Within the second portion of my book, *When God Commanded Build that Wall and The Evil Within*, I addressed the problem of evil in great detail. There I presented four arguments, as one would as a defense attorney, explaining why evil exists. You can also find those arguments by going to How to Defend Your Faith When Attacked[13] and 3 Powerful Defenses Against the Problem of Evil.[14]

3 Answers to the Problem of Evil

At the beginning of this chapter, we discussed how suffering actually plays a vital role in our learning obedience, establishing our faith, and discovering true joy. In the previous section, I presented a case for how a Sovereign, Loving God could ordain agonizing circumstances in life. I eluded to the "problem of Evil" which is an ongoing philosophical debate.

---

[13] https://www.myglorytoglory.com/blog/how-to-defend-your-faith-when-attacked

[14] https://www.myglorytoglory.com/blog/3-powerful-defenses-facing-problem-evil

Although, I am not among the brilliant minds that debate this issue; however, "the problem of evil" is an ideology for which I came to terms with long ago. Faith, with scholarly study lead me to embrace these 4 answers to the Problem of Evil.

The basic idea of the "Problem of Evil" is to say that A Sovereign Loving God could not have allowed evil's existence. Therefore, either God is not Sovereign, or He is not Loving. The Atheist loves to use this argument in an attempt to say God does not exist. But the truth is: He is Sovereign, He is Loving, and evil does exist.

As I previously pointed out, evil does not stand upon its own. In fact, could we even know, or could we quantify what is evil, were there not good. For evil is the absence of good. The shear fact that evil exists points to the truth that Righteousness, justice and truth must exist: which confirms God as creator. For no random conglomeration of molecules could have formed a moral compass. This is a topic for which I went into greater detail in *How to Defend God Against*

Secular Ideologies.[15] Now let's look briefly at the 4 Answers to the Problem of Evil.

1. Freedom of Will

    When God created mankind, He gave us all free will. His Sovereignty means that He remains fully in control of the affairs of men; however, His wisdom also saw that for love to be perfect-freedom to choose or not to choose Him was also necessary. This I realize is a point of extreme tension between the Calvinists and the Armenians. However, I believe as did C.S. Lewis and J.I. Packer that God's Absolute Sovereignty in the affairs of men is true, as also is true mankind's responsibility. Certainly, a dead spirit cannot choose God were God not to open their blinded eyes to see and desire Him, it is freely a gift of

---

[15]https://www.myglorytoglory.com/blog/defend-god-secular-ideologies

unmerited Grace. This means I have no "glory" or credit in having chosen to follow Him.

However, at the same time and equally true, God bids us to come and to evangelize that men might be saved. He warns us against the hardening of our own hearts. Of course, God knew that Adam would sin; yet, it is true that Adam chose to disobey God. Although, Adam walked in the garden every day with God, he did not truly value God's righteousness, glory, love or grace until after he had disobeyed and ate of the tree. Only then, did Adam see the magnificence of God in contrast to the evil apart from God's presence.

C. S. Lewis wrote in mere Christianity:

God created things which had free will. That means creatures can go either wrong or right. Some people think they can imagine a creature which was free but had no possibility of going wrong; I cannot. If a thing is free to be good it is also free to be bad. And free will is what has made evil possible. Why, then, did God give them free will? Because free will though it makes evil possible, is also the only thing that makes possible any love or goodness or joy worth having. A world of automata-of creatures that worked like machines-would hardly be worth creating.

The happiness which God designs for His higher creatures is the happiness of being freely, voluntarily united to Him and to each in an ecstasy of love delight compared with which the most rapturous love between a man and a woman on this earth is mere milk and water. And for that they must be free.[16] (C. Lewis 1952)

Without free will, we could never understand nor experience perfect love, joy, hope, or glory. Instead we would be like robots wandering about the planet with no depth of feeling and no reasoning. Lewis goes on to say:

"Of course, God knew what would happen if they used their freedom the wrong way: apparently, He thought it worth the risk. Perhaps we feel inclined to disagree with Him. But there is a difficulty about disagreeing with God. He is the source from which all your reasoning power comes: you could not be right, and He wrong any more than a stream can rise higher than its own source. When you are arguing against Him you are arguing

---

[16] C.S. Lewis, *Mere Christianity,* (New York: HarperCollins, 1952), 47-48

against the very power that makes you able to argue at all: it is like cutting off the branch you are sitting on. If God thinks this state of war in the universe a price worth paying for free will—that is, for making a live world in which creatures can do real good or harm and something of real importance can happen, instead of a toy world which only moves when He pulls the strings—then we may take it is worth paying."[17] (C. Lewis 1952)

Therefore, God was never the author of evil; yet, when given the freedom to choose, Adam chose sin through his own volition. Every human being since then is presented with the same choice. That we are free to choose; then, no longer can we blame God, rather it is our own choice. Indeed, God could have brought immediate judgment upon the earth; after all, He could see through the corridors of time all the

_____

[17] Lewis, *Christianity*, 47-48

evil that men and women would choose. However, He also could see through the corridors of time, everyone who would accept His gift of salvation. His overwhelming love for each and every one of them caused Him to stay His hand of judgment. He continues to steady His hand, today. Had He not, you nor I would be here to even discuss this.

He could have just turned His back upon the whole of creation. However, He did not do that either. Instead, He provided a way for man to choose Him through faith. From Genesis until now; God has provided a way for mankind to be saved from the evil within their own hearts and the world around them, through faith in Jesus Christ. The Old Testament looked forward to His coming by faith; and we, look back to see His completed work. As Paul presented in Romans, everyone is given a chose; because, God reveals Himself to each. Read Paul's defense:

For I am not ashamed of the gospel of
Christ: for it is the power of God unto

salvation to every one that believeth; .... For therein is the righteousness of God revealed from faith to faith: as it is written, the just shall live by faith. For the wrath of God is revealed from heaven against all ungodliness and unrighteousness of men, who hold the truth in unrighteousness; Because that which may be known of God is manifest in them; for God hath shewed it unto them. For the invisible things of him from the creation of the world are clearly seen, being understood by the things that are made, even his eternal power and Godhead; so that they are without excuse: Because that, when they knew God, they glorified him not as God, neither were thankful; but became vain in their imaginations, and their foolish heart was darkened. Professing themselves to be wise,

they became fools, who changed the truth of
God into a lie, and worshipped and served the
creature more than the Creator. (Romans
1:16-25).

Sovereignty Vs Prayer

I see the free will vs God's Sovereignty much as I do God's Sovereignty vs Prayer. Never am I not to pray earnestly, believing that prayer changes things. God commands as much. Yet, in that same moment I know God is Sovereign and already has a plan in place. His Omniscience already knows the answer. Just because, I am confined within this time/space continuum of humanity on earth does not negate that both are true at the same time with the same magnitude. "Faith is the substance of things hoped for and the evidence of things not seen" (Hebrews 11:1).

My salvation He orchestrated, planned, and carried out. 100% it was His grace and nothing that my guilty hands could have performed. He compelled my heart to desire and want Him. And now it is He who transforms my heart. Yet, each day He gives me the freedom to choose His word, His presence or to leave His love letters laying idle on the shelf. Even then, He will accomplish all that He has planned in my life. Much like the children of Israel who so often rebelled, worshipped idols, and walked away. Yet, that did not thwart God's plan that He would bring salvation through the seed of Abraham to all who would believe, both Jew and Gentile.

2. The Greater Good

The second defense is that of "the Greater Good" defense. As I presented at the beginning of this chapter and throughout the previous defense, evil serves a purpose; whether, we fully comprehend it or not. Augustine addressed it in this manner,

"For the Almighty God, who, as even the heathen acknowledge, has supreme power over all things, being Himself supremely good, would never permit the existence of anything evil among His works, if He were not so omnipotent and good that He can bring good even out of evil"[18] (Augustine 1961)

That has been precisely the case in my own life. Of a certainty, I would not fully know the joy, hope, and love which I experience now; had it not been for the trials I have faced in this journey. That I can confirm as truth also in the life of Pete and Mom. Every step of the way, God drew each of us nearer to Him. Pete was drawn into repentance unto salvation. Mom found faith, hope, and happiness now in Him. I found the sweetness of knowing His grace. Through it all, He provided me with glimpses of His Glory; while, at the same

---

[18] Augustine, *Enchiridion on Faith, Hope, and Love,* trans. J.F. Shaw, (Chicago: Henry Reguery, 1961), 11

time transforming my heart to love Him more. He sifted away the chaff, revealed the darkness and evil of my own selfish heart, and steadily worked at transforming me into the likeness of Christ. Though He has a lot more work to do in me, I realize how precious a thought it is that one day I will stand before Him with a heart like that of my Savior.

No one presents this truth with more clarity than does Joni Eareckson Tada. I would encourage you to go to YouTube and listen to any of her tapes. Particularly, I recommend her True Woman '14 Conference. In it she refers to suffering as God's lemon juice being squeezed over our hearts; transforming us. Also, she says; "there is no trial too great to face in order to know Jesus."

Or as Paul wrote:

For I reckon that the sufferings of this present time are not worthy to be compared with the glory which shall be revealed in us. (Romans 8:18)

Yea doubtless, and I count all things but loss for the excellency of the knowledge of Christ Jesus my Lord: for whom I have suffered the loss of all things, and do count them but dung, that I may win Christ (Philippians 3:8).

God has a purpose and a plan which is for our good. Evil exists in this world; yet, without it would I really know the ecstasy of knowing Jesus. Could I understand the magnitude of His goodness or righteousness if I had never seen the depravity that exists without Him. Only God can take a broken life, filled with wrong choices and still make it one filled with hope, love and joy.

3. For Our Joy and God's Glory

Ultimately, the existence of evil in this world was necessary for both our joy and God's Glory. It was presented by Jonathan Edwards and explains how it was necessary for our ultimate joy that God allow evil to exist in the world. I will let it stand upon its own merits; because, of all the defenses, this one was the one that shone light into my heart during many years of suffering. It provided me with a deeper understanding of my suffering and ultimately lead me to rejoice, even in my suffering. Jonathan Edwards wrote this with such clarity, that any attempt to explain it would demonstrate my own ineptness to express it as well. Here is what he wrote:

> "It is a proper and excellent thing for infinite glory to shine forth; and for the same reason, it is proper that the shining forth of God's glory be complete; that is, that all parts of his glory should shine forth, that every beauty should be proportionably effulgent (=radiant), that the beholder may have a proper notion of God. It is not proper that one glory should be exceedingly manifested, and another not at all....

Thus, it is necessary, that God's awful majesty, his authority and dreadful greatness, justice, and holiness, should be manifested. But this could not be, unless sin and punishment had been decreed; so that the shining forth of God's glory would be very imperfect, both because these parts of divine glory would not shine forth as the others do, and also the glory of his goodness, love, and holiness would be faith without them; nay, they could scarcely shine forth at all.

If it were not right that God should decree and permit and punish sin, there could be no manifestation of God's holiness in hatred of sin, or in showing any preference, in his providence, of godliness before it. There would be no manifestation of God's grace or true goodness, if there was no sin to be pardoned, no misery to be saved from. How much happiness so ever he bestowed, his goodness would not be so much prized and admired, and the sense of it not so great....

So, evil is necessary, in order to the highest happiness of the creature and the completeness of that communication of God, for which he made the world; because the creature's happiness consists in the knowledge of God, and the sense of his love. And if the knowledge of him be imperfect, the happiness of the creature must be proportionably imperfect."[19] (Edwards 1974)

Reread this argument, prayerfully; then, think about it when you are confronted with the problem of evil. I have

---

[19] Jonathan Edwards, "Concerning the Divine Decrees", *The Works of Jonathan Edwards,* (Edinburgh: Banner of Truth, 1974), 528

found this argument richly comforting to my soul. Its truth illuminated further when I consider what Paul wrote.

> *What if God, willing to shew his wrath, and to make his power known, endured with much longsuffering the vessels of wrath fitted to destruction: and that he might make known the riches of his glory on the vessels of mercy, which he had afore prepared unto glory* (Romans 9:22-23).

Lessons from God About Painful Suffering

Painful Suffering comes to us all at some time or another in this journey called life. Whether it be a broken heart, illness, fear of an unknown future, loss of a loved one, or despair. Life brings many challenges. Some are a result of our own choices, while others seem to appear out of nowhere.

Yet, the painful suffering that fills our heart, mind and spirit do come as we face this journey called life on this earth. However, there is a place of peace, hope and joy that can be found, even in the worst of circumstances.

Both Pete and Mom talked about the depth of painful suffering they endured in their bipolar world. They would tell me of a pain in their head. Not a headache. But a pain that overwhelmed them. Despite all the painful suffering I have faced in my own life, I must say it never could compare to theirs. Certainly, I faced moments of doubt, shame, and even moments of sorrow, fear, loneliness, or depression. Yet, I cannot say I ever endured the depth of painful suffering as did they. Theirs, at times, spilled over engulfing my life as well. Still, in the midst of it all, God had a perfect plan of love, grace and mercy for each one of us.

The Lord is close to the broken-hearted and saves those crushed by pain. (Psalm 34:18). In the midst of our painful suffering, He revealed Himself to each one of us.

Therein we each found these truths. The lessons of God learned through the pain and sorrow.

5 Lessons from God on Suffering

1. In this world, we will have painful suffering moments. Jesus said, "In this world ye shall have tribulation; but be of good cheer, I have overcome the world" (John 16:33). When Jesus prayed for us in John 17, He prayed to the Father to protect us, to give us His Joy, His Love, and His Glory. He did not ask that we be taken out of this world; but, that He give us His strength and peace as we face the painful trials that will be ours in this journey here on earth.

2. Through the painful suffering we face on this earth, our hearts are prepared to know Him. Could I know the wondrous refreshment of a cold glass of water, if I never experienced thirst? If I were satisfied with the things of this world, would I hunger and thirst for Him? Like C.S. Lewis wrote in *Mere Christianity.*

   "What Satan put into the heads of our remote ancestors was the idea that they could "be like gods"—could set up on their own as if they had

created themselves—be their own masters—invent some sort of happiness for themselves outside God, apart from God. And out of that hopeless attempt has come nearly all that we call human history—money, poverty, ambition, war, prostitution, classes, empires, slavery—the long terrible story of man trying to find something other than God which will make him happy. God cannot give us a happiness and peace apart from Himself, because it is not there. There is no such thing."
C. S. Lewis, Mere Christianity[20]

In the midst of our suffering, we come to see that we cannot find joy without Him. Yet, in our suffering we do find His Joy, His Strength, His Love, and His Grace to be sufficient to fill our hearts to overflowing.

3. In our painful suffering, we become more like Jesus.

I count all things but loss for the excellency of the knowledge of Christ Jesus my Lord: for whom I have suffered the loss of all things, and do count them but dung, that I may win Christ, and be found in Him. Not having a righteousness, which is of the law, but that which is through the faith of Christ, the righteousness which is of God by faith. That I may know Him, and the power of HIS SUFFERING, being made conformable unto His death. If by any means I might attain unto the resurrection of the dead. Not as though I

---

[20] C.S.Lewis, *Mere Christianity,*

had already attained, either were already perfect. But I follow after, if that I may apprehend that for which also I am apprehended of Christ Jesus. (Philippians 3: 8-12).

Whatever it takes to transform my heart to be like Him, I will gladly face. While at the same time I will trust His Hand of Love. After all He did for me, how could I do less?

4. God's plan for me is one of Grace, Mercy and Love. That means every detail of my life, He who knows what is best for me, has ordained it. Only He knows what is necessary or needed to transform my heart so that I might fully experience His Love, Peace, and Joy.

    Likewise, the Spirit also helpeth our infirmities. For we know not what we should pray for as we ought. But the Spirit, itself, maketh intercession for us with groanings which cannot be uttered. And He that searcheth the hearts knoweth what is the mind of the Spirit, because He maketh intercession for the saints according to the will of God. We know that all things work together for good to them that love God, to them who are called according to His purpose. For whom He did foreknow, He also did predestinate to be conformed to the image of His Son, that He might be the firstborn among many brethren. Moreover, whom He did predestinate, them He also called. And whom He called, them He also Justified. Whom He justified, them He also Glorified (Romans 8: 26:30).

Beloved, now are we the sons of God, and it doth not yet appear what we shall be: but we know that, when He shall appear, we shall be like Him; for we shall see Him as He is. (I John 3:2).

5. Our experience with painful suffering grows our faith.

    As I have so often referred to Hebrews ll:6. Faith is knowing that God IS and that He rewards those who diligently seek Him. If I know God is Sovereign, omnipotent, and loves me as He loves Jesus (John 17:23). Furthermore, He has promised to reward those who diligently seek Him, then, I know that even the painful suffering in my life are for my greater Joy. Even, when I don't understand, I can trust Him.

    *Therefore, being justified by faith, we have peace with God through our Lord Jesus Christ. By whom also we have access by faith into this **grace wherein we stand and rejoice in*** *hope of the Glory of God. And not only so, but we glory in tribulations also. Knowing that tribulation worketh patience and patience, experience; and experience hope. And hope maketh not ashamed; because, the love of God is shed abroad in our hearts by the Holy Ghost which is given unto us. (Romans 5:1-5).*

Concluding Thoughts Concerning our Painful Suffering

Whatever painful suffering that I, Mom, or Pete faced in this life, it has ultimately led to God. Therein, we each have found His Abiding, Steadfast Joy. Additionally, it has prepared us for an eternity with Him basking in His Love, Grace, and Mercy forever more.

From the Dark of the Night, for Mercy We Cry

From the Dark of the Night, for Your Mercy We Cry
As we look to the heavens and scream out, "Lord, Why?"
Why so much evil, such suffering and pain
Won't You reach down in Might, to this evil restrain
Before our dear nation doth fall like the rest
When we once had been known, as Christians, the best

"Look there around you, Oh, do you not see?
That You all have forgotten to focus on me
So, busy you run from life to and fro
While seeking great treasures and idols below
Have You forgotten I am the truth and the light?
Without me, there is only darkness of night!

When you shut out my presence all you will see
Is the evil remains in the absence of me!
How is it then, that you would forget?
I AM all you need for peace, love and joy; yet
You only seek me when your life is beset
By sorrows so filled with pain and regret

Did I not give my all, that you might be set free?

From the evil and pain that you find without me

You struggle through trials so filled with strife

While I stand here to offer you a new life

From the nothingness, darkness is all that you see

While being can only be found in me

I sent you my Son who died on a cross

To pay for your sins, at such a high cost

Because of my love, I gave you my best

That then within me you your heart could find rest

There can never be Grace without Justice, you see

For evil does reign in the absence of me

I cannot deny my righteousness, child

For evil would then unchained run a wild

It is an act of my grace, the earth does still spin

Awaiting one more heart for to win

Turn from your sins and seek me, my face

There you will find such perfect love, joy and grace

My Glorious King

My Sovereign Lord and King
Who joins me in my suffering
He's ever present at my side
That in His joy I might abide

My Glorious King hung on a cross
And never thought about His loss
By reason of His love for me
He paid my price, my penalty

So, willingly He left His throne
That I might never be alone
And when this life brings pain and tears
He's there to quiet all my fears

He took upon Himself my strife
To give to me eternal life
He cloaked me in His righteousness
That I might know His love and bliss

And on that cross His Glory shone

And ne'er a victim, did bemoan

His fate He chose with open arms

To free me from my own sin's harms

He rose again, oh Glorious Day

To bring me life and light the way

That ever present I might be

Wrapped in His love eternally

And thus, it is, I love Him so

That willingly I to must go

Where ever He would bid me to

For He is all that I pursue

He is the treasure that I seek

The strength I need, for I am weak

He is the love my heart desires

The only one my soul requires

Chapter 6:

Seeking Truth, Finding Forgiveness

Two people can witness the same incident. Yet, our memories see it and record it differently. So, how do we really find the truth? For me, growing up in a world with Mom's undiagnosed bipolar disorder, snippets of memories came to plague me at times. Recording of mom and dad's fights burned deep within. Additionally, words that injured my own pride over the years blasted within my heart and mind. More than anything, I wanted Mom and Dad to see that my heart was good. I wanted to be loved. Yet, my mind recorded each harsh word, while forgetting each sacrificial act of love. I could not see the truth of their love; although, now I can. What changed? How is it I can see the truth now, when I could not see it then?

Our human hearts are born with a desire to be exalted. We want others to see our goodness, deserving of love and respect. Obedience comes, at that point, from a desire to be exalted. Yet, that kind of obedience, always leads to frustration both within our family relationships and with our relationship to God. Instead, true obedience can only come from a heart of love, respect, and a desire to honor another above one's self. Truth opens our eyes to see the world through God's eyes, rather than our own. Until I could see the truth of my own self-exalting heart, I harbored anger in my heart. Though I would tell you I was the one who sacrificially forgave and loved Mom, the truth was far from that. God so graciously, patiently, and lovingly has step by step transformed my heart to see truth.

The Truth Shall Set You Free

Jesus said, "*If ye continue in my word, then are ye my disciples indeed; and ye shall know the truth, and the truth shall make you free*" (John 8:31-32). Certainly, He is speaking of the truth of the gospel which sets us free from the chains of sin. We must come to the truth knowing that we are sinners deserving of God's wrath. There is nothing within our self-exalting heart that can commend us to Him. *"All have sinned and come short of the Glory of God"* (Romans 3:23). Only by His Grace are we saved. *"For by Grace are ye saved through faith; and that not of yourselves: it is the gift of God: not of works, lest any man should boast"* (Ephesians 2:8-9).

The anger, pain, and hurt I felt toward Mom came because deep within I thought I deserved something more. It blinded me from seeing the truth of her love and sacrifice, along the way. How often do we do the same toward God? Even, though, we try to say that is not the case; however, the truth glares with that fact. Much like Elijah in I Kings 19, we sit and pout that I only have served You, Lord. I have fought for You. We expect some reward for having followed Him; but, the truth is our heart is so bent on our own self righteousness that we forget that it was grace alone that saved us. When we finally see our self for the wretched sinner that we are, then we shout with gratitude for every gift He has so graciously provided for us.

Think about all the times you have become angry against another. Dig deep within and ask yourself the hard question of why? Did you not take some word out of context? Or felt yourself more deserving than they? To lay aside and be freed from anger, we must first see the truth of our own self-centered heart.

Erasing Negative Tapes

If we try to analyze relationships, particularly within families, we will find that more often our anger is due to misperceptions of what was or is said. Then, our memories become packed full of negative tapes which play back in our heads, whenever we are around that person. Whatever they say, we then hear through an already prejudiced mindset, adding fuel to the flame. We put up walls and barriers which are in place to protect our self, we think. But the truth is those walls and barriers only cause further harm by allowing anger, loneliness, and bitterness to grow.

The evolutionist will try to tell you that our brains choose to record that which is necessary for survival first. However, as I just pointed out, were that the case then evolution failed in its purpose. We can see that clearly in a society who is bent on emotions of anger, hatred, and separationist ideologies that ultimately lead to high anxiety, desperation, drug abuse, and even suicide. All because the memory held fast to negative tapes, snippets of information taken out of context which ignore the good and misinterpret the words to feed a negative narrative.

Paul wrote in Philippians 4:8-9 *"Finally, brethren, whatsoever things are true, whatsoever things are honest, whatsoever things are just, whatsoever things are pure, whatsoever things are lovely, whatsoever things are of good report; if there be any virtue, and if there be any praise, think on these things. Those things, which ye have both learned,*

147

and received, and heard, and seen in me, do: and the God of peace shall be with you. "

Negative Tapes that Lead to Anger

For me, from the first memories I could recall, my mind created negative tapes of words spoken critically or harshly. My emotions would bounce between love, wanting to be loved, and building unhealthy walls. Perhaps, it was in part due to my sensitivity to mom's struggles which carried her from anger to depression to brief moments of joy. She had not yet been diagnosed; but, some of the characteristics of her bipolar were there. At any rate, I seemed to be also caught within the pendulum of wanting to find a way to make her happy and frustration when I failed. As time went by, in self-defense of my own bruised ego; my mind recorded negative tapes.

By holding fast to these negative words, I could defend my bruised ego by placing all the blame on Mom. Ah, but with time there was the anger inside that grew. Then, I hated myself for the anger, which I knew was wrong. The anger stood in the way of my being able to see all the acts of sacrificial love and kindness from Mom toward me. Instead, I worked always harder to prove that I WAS the kind, loving, and sacrificial one. What a mess was my little self-exalting heart. Yet, God was gracious, kind, patient, and loving toward this rebellious little heart. He knew that for me to find His peace in the relationship between myself and mom, He would have to erase the negative tapes one by one. Those negative tapes would have to be replaced with the truth, as only God could reveal.

Replacing the Negative Tapes with Truth

God is truth. With the guidance of the Holy Spirit, through studying God's Word and prayer, we can find the truth of even our relationships. We must learn, step by step, to see life through His eyes. Coming to the end of our self, we find His victory in every step of our life. God would bring every negative tape to the surface again, so that He could reveal to me the truth. Overtime, He erased all the negative tapes. Finally, I could see Mom through the eyes of love that God had for her. Also, finally, I could see all the sacrifice and love she had always given for me. Furthermore, Mom for the first time ever, is happy, peaceful and content. Where did she find that contentment? God and God alone. She has found her joy in sitting alone with Him, reading His word, and many good books about Him.

We need to learn to think on those things which are pure, kind, and good as we take our eyes off self and place them on Jesus. As we lay aside the self-exalting, sin filled nature of our humanity and find our self in Him alone, then the negative tapes will all fade away. Instead, we will find His truth, His joy, His peace, and His love reigning in our hearts.

How the Truth of God Softens Hearts to Forgive

Whenever we find ourselves in a situation where we are filled with angry frustration, we need to stop to analyze why Because if we don't, we will find our words and deeds demonstrating un-Christlike behavior. Unfortunately, when this happens, typically we excuse ourselves for not being able to forgive someone. We may even try to say that our anger is justified as righteous indignation. After all, we proclaim "they hurt us so deeply that we believe we have the right to be angry." We blurt out words meant to hurt or injure them in the same manner we believe they have hurt us. Furthermore, we search for evidences to prove that we are right in our anger and bitterness. We may even pray and try to lay the anger at the cross, seeking forgiveness; yet, within the next few hours, once more, the evidence of our unforgiving heart blurts out some statement or proof defending our anger. Pride stands in the way of our seeing the truth. Only the truth of God can soften our hearts and teach us to forgive. Yet, too often we don't want to hear the truth; because, we will find our own selfish pride makes us guilty.

When more cruel words pour from our lips; we recognize that we have not truly dealt with the issue yet. Instead we have only tried to cover it up. We realize that deep within the recesses of our heart there stands a much bigger issue that we have not dealt with. So, perhaps, the better question would be instead of what do we do; what can I do that will result in my fulfilling Ephesians 4?

Ephesians 4: [31] *Let all bitterness, and wrath, and anger, and clamour, and evil speaking, be put away from you, with all malice:*[32] *And be ye kind one to another, tenderhearted, forgiving one another, even as God for Christ's sake hath forgiven you.*

We need desperately to go back to the beginning and allow God to open our eyes, asking the Holy Spirit to reveal truth to our hearts, even if that means we must accept our own guilt in the broken relationship.

Learning God's Truth to Forgive Mom

The truth of God needed to soften my heart to unlock the negative tapes and teach me how to forgive Mom. Within the relationship of mom and me, I needed a lot of help. Conflicted by the hidden anger which came from stuffing my emotions, God worked with great patience to soften my heart. Why was this so much harder? A greater divide stood in the way; because, I was unwilling and unable to recognize the problem inside myself. Furthermore, I blinded myself to all the sacrificial unconditional love mom had shown me; because, then I would have to accept my own guilt and accept my own life's bad choices for what they really were: my failures. It is so much easier to overlook my own sins, if I could blame Mom.

God began to work in me through my relationship with Pete. Therein, He taught me how true love does forgive. True love, like Christ's, is unconditional. As I learned to forgive Pete and love him unconditionally, God guided my spiritual growth. This came over time, as the Holy Spirit opened my heart and mind to see Pete's heart through God's eyes. Pete's heart was kind, generous and beautiful; but, very broken. His life story was filled with pain, sorrow, and suffering which had lead to his deep seated sorrow.

Miraculously, God taught me of His unconditional love by filling my heart with unconditional love. Willingly, I forgave Pete; because, God would reveal to me the heart of Pete and the conflicts he faced in his bipolar world. This was step one; but, God knew it would take even more to soften my heart toward Mom. Although I could see the root cause of Pete's moments of violence, I needed to translate that into the same ability to forgive Mom for words that hurt and played within my mind.

Trials at Work: How to forgive.

As we already looked at in previous chapters, I have struggled with the need to feel loved, the need to feel validated, and the need to feel that at least at something I was good. That need drove me further. It stood out as a motivating factor in my life. In some ways that was good; because it drove me to strive harder and to succeed at work. However, as with everything it becomes a matter of the heart whether that is truly good, or it turns into self-exalting, prideful behaviors.

I worked very hard to succeed at work. Whatever task was placed in my hands I marched forward and asked

God for His guidance and strength, recognizing it was not my own strength that could accomplish it. When did that turn from being a mission for God into something that I clung to with all my soul? I can't tell you. Perhaps I would have never known that it had changed; until one day God ripped the secure position I thought was my stronghold from my grasping hands.

My position at work was suddenly changed. I became frightened, angry, frustrated, and felt betrayed. I wanted to find someone to blame; someone for whom I could be angry. I plunged deep into my heart to try to understand this anger; because, I knew that anger could not be a part of who I am in Christ and could cause harm to the name of Christ. I needed to find those dark spots in my heart so that God's light could shine into them, dispelling their power.

Truth Softens My Heart

At first, I did not realize it was God who ripped my position of prestige from my hands. Remembering the truth of Romans 8:28 I told myself that if God is in control and His plan was to make all things work together for good; then this was part of His Plan for my life. So, I began to pray desperately to remove the anger and please not allow this to hurt my testimony for Him. I would think finally I had conquered this when suddenly out of nowhere came angry thoughts or snide words. Ok, so there must be something much deeper I needed to identify.

I began a nightly journey in which I asked God to reveal the source. There it was, I had replaced my only true source of joy (God) with a counterfeit joy in my work. I had begun to believe that my protection, my sense of being loved, and my security were found in my job; rather, than truly trusting God whenever the counterfeit joy seemed to

157

slip from my hands. I delved into the scripture once more to cling tight to my only hope which was grounded in the covenant promises of God who was the one who loved me, provided for me, and protected me. Then, I began the arduous task of erasing all the negative tapes and replacing them with those of virtue and kindness.

Back to Mom and Me

So, God spent years revealing to me truth about myself and my own heart. He did this through many trials. Still, He needed to bring me full circle and back to Mom. As time went by, I began to remember tidbits of truth. How mom had always sacrificed and loved me unconditionally. When I came home, divorced at the age of 19—Mom was right there. She did not condemn or criticize me for being a failure. In fact, she said it was her fault for having pushed me into marriage. Indeed, she always just wanted the best for me. She wanted me to find love, marriage and a good home where God could be central. There was the time I came home with Melissa, after my second divorce. Again, she was there with open arms.

After Pete's death, she bought me a house. When I went back to school, she every day came to the house to make certain my sons had breakfast and dinner prepared with their laundry done. Then, when I had cancer, she was there to help me whenever I needed her both financially and physically. Why was it that my mind had clung to every negative word and forgotten the truth of her sacrificial love? Perhaps it was my own self-exalting heart trying to shift my sins and my guilt onto the one person who had sacrificed the most to love me.

Even the hurtful words that spewed from Mom on rare occasion had been her own pain, caused by my failure to recognize her love for me. I realize now how little I said thank you for all she did.

But God did not leave it there. In His Sovereign design, Mom needed me and came to live with me for more than 10 years. During those years, we had good times and bad; however, in the end came to realize the depth of love we each had for the other. Mom was always there for me and I for her. That is the truth of our story. In the end there was nothing to be forgiven, there is only the love between us that bound our hearts always together throughout a lifetime.

How to Overcome the Pride Causing Unforgiveness

Jesus has called us to love one another, even as Jesus Christ loved us. (John 13:34). He loved the Pharisee who spit on his face, the roman guard who beat Him, His brother who called Him crazy and those who stood to mock Him at the foot of the cross. In His most painful moments on the cross He prayed, *"Father forgive them, for they know not what they are doing"* (Luke 23:24). Jesus came as a humble servant to serve and to die that we, deserving of death might live (Matthew 20:28). Angry, unforgiving spirits have no place in the life of a believer who fully understands that their own forgiveness came at such a price. When we lay aside the Pride Causing Unforgiveness, only then can we love as Jesus loved.

So, what are the steps to erasing the negative tapes playing in your head?

1. **Plunge**

   deep into the recesses of your heart to locate those areas of darkness locked away. Those areas you don't want exposed, even to God. Perhaps you are afraid that if God saw the depth of covetousness, the desires for self-exaltation, He wouldn't be able to love you anymore. The truth is…He already knows every thought and every blemish of your heart; and, yet, He has chosen to love you. Psalm 69: *5"O God, thou knowest my foolishness; and my sins are not hid from thee."*

Often, it is there where we have hidden some painful memory which we have capped so tightly that we think we have hidden it from ourselves; but, it sits waiting to explode into our current situations. Ask God to help you recognize it so that God can gently take it, covering you with His love while you weep in His arms until the pain goes away.

2. Remember

that God is on His Throne. Nothing can happen within the Christian's life but what it has been either ordained by God or has been allowed by His Sovereign will. Given that truth and God's promise that *all things work together for good to those who love God* (Romans 8:28); then, no matter what the circumstance appears, God has a plan working for good in our lives.

Sometimes that plan is to sift us, removing the chaff that remains in our hearts. His purpose is to make us look more like Christ. There are things within us that may require pain to remove them. There are things that need to be purified by fire. While we attempt to hold tightly to these counterfeit joys, He needs to burn away our pride, so that we become more like Christ.

3. **Identify**

what is the true source of your distress with the issue. That is sometimes a laborious task and can only occur as we ask God to reveal it to us. I guarantee you that whenever we feel hurt or wronged it comes from a deeper problem within our own heart than whatever the perceived offence is. And, yes, I said perceived.

Most of the time it is our perception. While the reality is that the other person never meant to cause harm; but were themselves trying to deal with deeper trials or desires of their own. Generally, our response comes from fear (a lack of faith), recollections of painful moments from our past, reactions to unresolved past conflicts with someone else that we have stuffed into the darkest recesses of our heart. *"for of the abundance of the heart his mouth speaketh."* Luke 6:45

4. Delve

into the scriptures to grasp hold of the covenant promises of God and cling to them. I am certain that in step three you will discover that there are issues which you have never by faith accepted God's promise to cover.

Sin is always evidence of a faith issue. Do you really believe all that God has said? If that were true, you could never be anxious, unruffled, sorrowful, or affected by the circumstances that surround you; instead, you would have peace, joy, hope, and love which continuously reflects Glory back to God as a mirror reflecting to the world His Glory (not your own.) *"But without faith it is impossible to please him: for he that cometh to God must believe that he is, and that he is a rewarder of them that diligently seek him."* Hebrews 11:6

5. **Erase**

the negative audio tapes that play in your head and replace them with new tapes. You know which tapes I am talking about. Follow Paul's directions when replacing those tapes with new ones. *"whatsoever things are lovely, whatsoever things are of good report; if there be any virtue, and if there be any praise, think on these things"* Philippians 4:8

There you have it, if you take the first letters of each word you will find the word PRIDE. You might say; but mine is not pride I am struggling with doubt and a low self-esteem? Isn't that also pride? Do you think that you are so important that your mistakes, self-frustrations, sins are too big for God to forgive or to take care of?

Sometimes, self-doubt is a form of backwards pride because doubt keeps me focused on myself and not on my Savior. When focused on my self-doubt or desires I become preoccupied by myself. I forget that my life in Christ is not about me. It is about a world in need of a Savior. God needs me to reflect His Glory, His Love, and His Joy to a desperate world. He does that as His Truth softens my heart and teaches me to forgive.

WHEN TRUTH SETS US FREE FROM PRIDE

. What a patient, gentle, and loving Father I have. He has a plan for my life and I trust Him to finish the work He has begun in me. I could now fulfill Ephesians 4: 31-32; at least for today until some other piece of chaff needs to be sifted and I must walk through these steps again. Knowing this, *"Brethren, I count not myself to have apprehended: but this one thing I do, forgetting those things which are behind, and reaching forth unto those things which are before, I press toward the mark for the prize of the high calling of God in Christ Jesus."* Philippians 3: 13-15.

So, what stands in your way of fulfilling Ephesians 4: 31-32. Read the verse again, now that you know the steps to guide you toward fulfilling it.

Ephesians 4: 31-32, Let *all bitterness, and wrath, and anger, and clamour, and evil speaking, be put away from you, with all malice: And be ye kind one to another, tenderhearted, forgiving one another, even as God for Christ's sake hath forgiven you.*

One by one God removed the prideful negative tapes I clung to. Then, I saw the sacrificial love Mom had always shown toward me. Even in my worst moments, she had loved me unconditionally. I know that now.

What is Truth?

Often in our society, people will try to say that what is true is relative to how we, as a society, choose to believe. We are told that justice, goodness, morality all are relative to our social norms at the time; based very much upon our feelings. Yet, if that were the case, nothing is true, and everything is relative. In that scenario, relativity itself is relative. Basing truth upon my own inner compass or societies compass, can lead to constant fluctuations, chaos, and social norms based on the lie that "I" am the most important. How I feel at any given moment becomes the basis of what is true for me. But can that be truth?

In fact, did not Hitler lead an entire society to believe in the superiority of their ideologies, making genocide of the

Jews a good thing. He truly believed this to be true; but, alas we know the horror of that reliance on self to determine what is right.

The terrorists who plunged an airplane into the twin towers believed what they were doing was for the better good of all. They gave their own lives in the process for what they thought was true.

So, if truth is relative, then how can we ever condemn the atrocities of slavery, injustice, murder, terror, or abuse? There must be that which is true and that which is false, for without truth there can be no compass. The same must be true in my daily decisions and with my relationships. If there is one thing I learned through living with Mom and Pete in their bipolar worlds, it is this: I cannot rely on my own emotional compass to determine or know what is true. Instead, I would need to seek truth outside of me from the only true source of all truth: God.

3 Lessons from God on Truth

1. Humanity's Compass is Broken

The heart is deceitful above all things, and desperately wicked: who can know it? (Jeremiah 17:9). By nature, because of sin, all of us are born with the belief that we are the center of this universe. Perpetuated even further by modern philosophies, we tend to see the world through our pride filled, self-exalting eyes. This distorts all that is true into whatever illusion makes us look good at whatever cost to others. The self-preservation lies we devise then becomes what we believe of our world. That leads to anger, bitterness, and isolation at times. It leads to "I am right, you are wrong" mentality.

2. God is True (Jeremiah 10:10, John 3:33, 17:3)

If I am to know what is true, I must first seek Him. To prove this fact to the unbeliever, would take more than

I have time to write in this section. However, for the moment I can stand upon this truth as did C.S. Lewis. *I believe in Christianity as I believe that the sun has risen: not only because I see it, but because by it I see everything else.* In Him, I have found peace, love, hope, and joy; none of which I could find on my own.

3. **Only God can Transform Our Hearts**

Through faith in Jesus Christ, seeking Him first, my heart is transformed into one that sees the world through His eyes. My transformation continues as I seek Him through reading His word and prayer. Never would I desire to go back to relying on my own broken compass. If only you knew the freedom of loving; because, He first loved you. Therein lies what is true.

FORGIVENESS

Oh, Lord, how does this bleeding heart

So gripped with pain, forgiveness give

For acts that ripped my soul apart

By all they said and all they did

Your Joy, dear Lord, they stole from me

Confusion, chaos fills my mind

Only you can set me free

That I might stand and Thy light shine

So, take me back unto that cross

My selfish acts, your bleeding heart

That I might truly know Your loss

Forgiveness came at what a cost.

If I could see me as I am

Compared to perfect righteousness

So undeserving of this lamb

Who gave the final sacrifice

Oh, then Dear Lord I'd see mankind

Through eyes, your eyes filled with Your Love

Forgiving Spirit then I'd find

For every act, for every word

Please, let me have this heart of Yours

To reach a bitter world in pain

So, joy, and love and peace outpours

To shine Your light of hope again.

Forgiveness comes from a humble heart who has taken the
time to look from the outside in. When we see our
own frailties, it is easier to forgive others theirs.

Chapter 7:

Learning of Love

Love can be such a mystery. It can raise our hearts to the highest peaks of joy and hope. Miraculously, it can give us strength to keep going through the toughest of circumstances. Yet, at the same time, it can bring us the greatest pain and sorrow. However, of all the emotions we face as humans, love can be the most difficult to fully understand. For me, it is love that most points to the truth of Gods existence. It cannot be explained by the evolutionist. Love is the greatest gift God gave His creation. Yet, it is the area of greatest brokenness in this fallen world. I John 4:8 tells us, *He that loveth not knoweth not God, for God is Love.*

For God so loved the world that He gave His only begotten son, that whosever believeth in Him should not perish, but have everlasting life John 3:16.

We are born with a need for love, as well as a desire to love and be loved. Often it drives us, pushes us, and even breaks us. Yet, do we really understand love?

In Search of Love

On February 15, 2016, I began a series on my blog site entitled In Search of Love. Throughout that series, I, with great vulnerability, told my readers of the story of my life. Therein, I honestly wrote of all the good, the bad, the ugly and the beauty discovered in my search for true love.

In John 17, Jesus prayed to God, the Father. As I wrote in *Abiding, Steadfast Joy,* within this prayer of Jesus it is revealed the purpose for which God created us. Therein, we discover that first and foremost, it was His overwhelming love that caused Him to create us. The love between the Father and Son so great, as the Son being the perfect echo of the Father. Both being one in perfect righteousness, holiness, and sovereignty. The Holy Spirit, also being God, is the outpouring of that love. Our highest point of elation in love is only miniscule in comparison to the love embodied within the Triune God. That love was so great that it could not be contained, but, rather overflowed. God created us that His overflowing love might have a vessel upon which to pour forth. In other words, He created us to experience and be filled with the Joy of His love.

To fully experience that depth of love meant we would not only be recipients of His love; but that we might know the joy of loving Him. We could not know that kind of love toward Him, if we were not given the freedom to love. Without being given the choice to love Him, we could never know the truth and depth of love.

Loved as the Son is Loved

Furthermore, as Jesus spoke to the Father in John 17:22-23, He said, *"And the glory which thou gavest me I have given them; that they may be one, even as we are one: I in them, and thou in me, that they may be made perfect in*

177

one; and that the world may know that thou hast sent me, and hast loved them, as thou hast love me."

Did you get that? God has loved me and you with the same depth of love that He loved His Son. How can that be? Still, there it is! So, let me ask you. Are you in search of love? Jesus Christ is standing there with open arms to embrace you and to fill you with a love beyond measure.

For this cause I bow my knees unto the Father of our Lord Jesus Christ, of whom the whole family in heaven and earth is name, that He would grant you, according to the riches of His glory to be strengthened with might by His Spirit in the inner man. That Christ may dwell in your hearts by faith; that ye, being rooted and grounded in love, May be able to comprehend with all saints what is the breadth, and length, and depth and height. And to know the love of Christ, which passeth knowledge, that ye might be filled with all the fulness of God. (Ephesians 3:14-19).

Do You Really Know the Magnitude of God's Love?

I am fully convinced that if we ever fully grasped the magnitude of God's love for each of us, we would never worry, doubt, fret, experience fear, or even know sorrow. Imagine this, the God who created all the heavens and earth and who reigns Sovereign over all His creation, loves you and wants to shower you with His love, His joy, and His glory. He who knows all things, is working together everything, so that your heart can experience the maximum of joy for all of eternity with Him. Every miniscule detail of your life, He has been there. Each tear, He has earnestly longed to wipe away, desiring that you comprehend that even the tears came because He loved you. Wrapped within each tear came a lesson in truth that drew your heart closer to His Heart, wherein rest and solace could be found.

Oh, yes; I am convinced that if I ever fully grasped the magnitude of God's love for me, I would soar above the trials and worries of this life. A peaceful smile of delight and joy would cover my face. Strength would emerge to claim victory over every task I face. Wisdom would guide every choice I make, as I fully rely upon His word. Resting and abiding in Jesus Christ, I would allow the power of the Holy Spirit to perform His work in and through me. If only I fully understood the magnitude of God's love for me: the breadth, the length, the depth, and the heighth thereof. What could I ever fear!

The problem is and has always been, this human heart of mine does not invariably grasp the magnitude of His love for me. At times, I forget, doubt, or underestimate His love.

Rooted and Grounded in His Love

Paul's prayer was that each believer know the power of the Holy Spirit in their lives. Jesus Christ died that we might be redeemed. The same power that raised Him from the dead indwells each and every believer who has accepted Jesus Christ as their Lord and Savior. We are to be rooted and grounded in the magnitude of God's love toward us. What could that mean?

First, to be rooted in His love refers to where we get the source of our nourishment. Just as the Bible tells us that we are the branches; but, He is the vine. We are to abide in Him. But, how does a tree or vine gain strong roots? Those trees with the strongest and deepest roots have faced moments of drought forcing them to dig deeper. Or it may have faced extreme storms with gale force winds that forces the roots to dig deeper into the soil. Moments of drought and storms enter our lives that our roots may dig deeper into the source of our strength, Jesus Christ and His love for us.

Grounded refers to our foundation. Where is your foundation? Is it built upon the truth of God's word or upon the words of men? If we build upon a foundation of human thoughts and ideas, our house will crumble when winds blow. Our foundation of love cannot be based on human philosophy and feel good ideas of self-exalting men and women. If love is to stand, it must be built upon God's word. His word is true. I cannot understand or begin to grasp the magnitude of God's love for me, if I never read His word.

The Magnitude of God's Love on Display

Read God's Word. From Genesis to Revelation, the magnitude of God's love is on display. Within each story, look for it. God's Love and Grace sustained humanity; despite, their foolishness, pride and sin. Certainly, His Righteousness and Justice would demand payment for sin. Yet, He willingly even paid the price that all who would accept His gift of salvation, by faith would be saved. Even His most faithful of servants failed at times. But God always remained faithful, fulfilling His promise to them. He showed His mercy, grace, and love. The magnitude of God's love forgave sin, as He guided each life into a deeper knowledge of His love. He transformed each willing heart, transforming their life until it became rooted and grounded in His love. As their reliance on Him grew, their faith grew. They became strengthened by the Holy Spirit to do great and mighty things.

As you study the Word of God, you will discover that for each faithful servant, God was willing to use a lifetime of trials to teach them of the magnitude of God's love for them. Furthermore, you will discover that each grew in strength, joy, hope and faith. Therefore, I must say, I have been so blessed to have faced all that I have. Also, Mom would tell you the same. Just to know Him and the power of His word. To know the magnitude of God's love toward me, and the power of His might within me. Oh, I am not fully transformed; but, I am being changed day by day through the work of the Holy Spirit.

Chapter 8:

Can Broken People Love Unconditionally?

Within our relationships, we come broken, carrying baggage. Needing to uphold our fragile self-image, we bring all our brokenness to the relationship in hopes to be repaired. Our needs outweigh our ability to love unconditionally another just for who they are. Often, our "loving" someone is dependent upon how they make us feel about ourselves. In other words, we love ourselves more than we truly love the other person in the relationship. It is no wonder we live in a society where relationships are broken, divorce is rampant, and family arguments rip siblings and parents apart. Furthermore, we see the divisions in society, where everyone is screaming so loudly against each other rather than to allow grace and civility to reign. Because of sin, we are a broken people. So, is there any hope that we can learn to love unconditionally, as God does?

Precisely, that was the problem within my relationship with mom. I was more concerned with "how I felt" than in seeing the beauty of who she is in God's eyes. Even when I strove, sacrificially, to do things to bring her joy, I was thinking of me. Of course, I wanted to feel better about me. Or perhaps, to declare myself a "saint" by my actions. Only God, can transform us from the inside out and give us a new heart of understanding, grace and unconditional love toward other flawed and broken people. We are all broken because of sin.

Learning to Love Unconditionally

Miraculously, in my life, God used another individual suffering from bi-polar to open my eyes so that I could learn to love Mom unconditionally. As God transformed my heart to love Pete unconditionally, He opened my heart to see

186

everything differently. I also began to understand the love unconditionally that God's grace afforded me. *"But God commandeth His love toward us, in that, while we were yet sinners, Christ died for us"* (Romans 5:8). As I learned to trust in God's love for me, my heart transformed so that I could love others for who they are, not merely how they make me feel about myself.

That does not mean that I love sin; but it does mean I love the sinner. Sometimes, that means in gentle humility, I speak the truth and stand in defense of the abused and down trodden. But I do so from a heart desiring to spread the gospel message to a broken dying world.

My greatest gift, most precious treasure is Jesus Christ. If I truly unconditionally love the world as Christ did, then I want to share that treasure with everyone I meet. Knowing that the only hope, joy, and true love humanity can find are found in a relationship with God, through faith in Jesus Christ, then, I must shout His name from the rooftops. To do so; however, requires my life also be an example of His love. I must die to my selfish desire for self-exaltation. Only when I come to the end of me, can His love unconditionally shine through me to others. That is why Jesus said, "*If any man will come after me, let him deny himself, take up his cross daily and follow me*" (Luke 9:22-24). Daily I must die to self; because, this human heart so tries to revive itself to take the throne that belongs to Christ alone.

How to Really Love with God's Heart

With all the brokenness within our human heart, how do we learn to really love with God's Heart. He who saw the darkest crevices of my self-exalting sin of pride, the filthy rags I chose to adorn myself, still loved me unconditionally and pursued me relentlessly. Choosing me to be His own, even knowing every time I would stumble and fail in my futile attempts to love Him as I should. How often did I fail to bring glory to His name? Or how often did I bemoan His plan, somehow thinking I knew better than He what was best for me? There was a time, I asked why it was my entire life had been providing care for those with bipolar disorder. Why was there no one to care for me? So, foolish I was! For now, I see how truly blessed I have been. God has been there every step of the way, wrapping me within His arms of love and providing all I needed.

Mom and Pete battled a disease I could not fully comprehend. I must confess there were times when my heart cried out, "Why can't you get it together? Everyone faces moments of depression and moments of joy. Just put one foot in front of the other and try harder. That is what I have to do." There were moments when their critical words blurted out unfiltered and cut deep into my soul. I wanted to cry out in despair. For Pete, his disease also came with moments of violent, uncontrollable rage as he reached the peak of mania, just before he plummeted into a deep, dark suicidal depression. I became entrapped in this rollercoaster of emotions with him. From love to fear to sorrow, I was the one who had to be strong; but, knew deep within, I wasn't. Still, God was there allowing my heart to forgive and to grow in both strength and love. It was God's who allowed every detail of my life, that I might learn to rely on Him.

Learning to Love

I pleaded with God at times to release my heart. Instead, each time I begged to be freed from the love that bound me to Pete and Mom; He opened a window for me to understand their pain. At first, I felt more trapped. I would cry out to God, "I can't do this. You've got the wrong girl, God." Then, step by step, through His strength, I kept moving forward. My feeble arms and legs would gain strength, moving through one moment at a time. Pete found Jesus Christ as his Savior before he died. God's plan was the salvation of one soul for all of eternity. At the same time, God opened my eyes to see that there was no pain too great to suffer for the salvation of one soul.

What I suffered was nothing compared to what Christ had suffered for my salvation. After all, I was broken, a sinner undeserving of His Grace; yet, He loved me just the same. Inch by inch, God had taught me how to really love Pete. He had taught me to see Pete and to love him in a way that displayed God's heart to him. Something, I could not have done on my own. In fact, I can tell you of all the times I failed to do just that. But, God in His great mercy shone through me to reach out to Pete, irrespective of my own failures and flaws. Then, on January 15, 1994, Pete accepted Christ as his Savior. On July 23, 1994, Pete died. Certainly, that was not the ending my heart desired. I just wanted him healed, so that I might also reap the joy of his love for me. But that was not God's plan, as I explained in the introduction to *Abiding, Steadfast Joy*.

God's Heart

Next God needed to mend the brokenness that remained between Mom and me. There was so much more I had to learn. After Pete's death, I returned home. Living near Mom, all the negative defensive tapes I had recorded came flooding in. Well, there were even new ones that came to add to my collection. During those years, I battled widowhood, being a single parent to teenage sons who had already faced too much pain in their own lives. Soon thereafter, I battled breast cancer, followed by ulcerative colitis. Focused on my own struggles, I could not see the sacrifice of Mom's love for me. With all that I had learned, I had so much still to learn.

Seeking the Truth in Love and Forgiveness

With all that I had learned of love and forgiveness during the years I lived with Pete, one would think that truth would permeate all the areas of my life. However, it did not. God, in His wisdom, continued to work on my heart through circumstances, trials, and lessons from Him.

As I previously mentioned, after Pete's death, I returned home. During the first months, I traveled back and forth from Mexico. Completing the tasks set before me, I left the children with Mom. One month in Mexico, one month in Missouri; I made the arduous three-day drive from Pachuca to Dexter alone. Emotionally, mom struggled with the task. Instead of truly understanding her struggle, I was frustrated by it. Right before I was able to make my final move to Missouri, I lost half of all my money in the 1994 crash of the Mexican markets. Mom rushed out and bought me a home. Instead of seeing this act of sacrificial love and kindness, I became obsessed with her words. She said, "I bought the house because I could not imagine having to live with you and your children."

Yes, Mom sometimes blurted out words without thought. But if I had forgiven Pete his moments of violence through understanding, why was it harder to forgive Mom for words.

More Lessons in Love and Forgiveness

Then, in 1997, I decided to go to Vanderbilt to seek my master's Degree in Nursing. The children and I discussed it at length before I made that decision. I would travel from Dexter to Nashville on Sunday, stay in the dorm, and return on Friday. Mom would come over and cook their breakfast, do their laundry and have dinner on the table. I called every evening. My sons were more mature than most their age, so I trusted them. Besides it was a small town, our house was nestled between the homes of a lawyer and an older woman who would have told me if anything was going on.

November 1998, I was diagnosed with a very aggressive form of breast cancer. How gracious God is. Now looking back, whenever I would question my decision to go to school, I know that the cancer which was hidden would not have been found if I had not been at Vanderbilt. Nor would I have been in a trial study which proved the curing factor, were it not for my being at Vanderbilt. Every step of the way, God controlled the details of my life. He also placed me in the position where I needed Mom's help, even if I did not want to admit it.

School, chemo, and all its battles completed. My sons both off to study, I then had an unusually aggressive form of ulcerative colitis that did not respond to the high dose steroids and constant medications. Ultimately, I had my colon removed. For one month, I lived with a very unruly ileostomy that awakened me each morning with a broken bag. One morning, feeling so very alone at 4 am, shivering in bed, trying to get a new bag on after a shower; I called Mom who came running over to help. She always came when I needed her.

Intertwining Our Lives, God's Grace

How could I not fully see her sacrifice? In truth, I did; but, a part of my selfish pride did not. Having finally gotten past the cancer, the ulcerative colitis, and the surgeries; I decided to move 4 hours away. Again, I allowed a new tape to play in my head. At one moment of frustration, mom had said, "I will be so glad when you and your children are gone so I can just rest and do what I want." So, off I went to my new job and new life, feeling vindicated in my leaving because of her words. Six months later, Mom had a complete emotional breakdown and I moved her to Springfield to be near me.

After searching all the available independent living facilities, I chose the best, brightest and newest I could find.

A part of me wanted so much for Mom to be happy with my choices. Yet, she would tell everyone, I took everything from her. When I asked her why, she would tell me that she liked people to feel sorry for her.

When in 2003, I moved to Florida; I moved mom in with me. For the next 13 years, we lived together. There were moments when her medications would require adjustments. Other times, she would end up in the hospital in a psychiatric ward. I just wanted her to be happy; but I wanted to prove myself by being the source of that happiness. A very foolish, self-centered love; not, true love and forgiveness as God had shown me. Yet, step by step God was chipping away the stony bits of my heart. Mom can no longer be left alone throughout the day and requires more care. She is now in a nursing home. However, I now see her for the woman of strength, courage, and sacrificial love she truly is. God had finally transformed my heart to know the truth of love and forgiveness; although, it took a lifetime.

Mom is and has always been my best friend, my greatest advocate, and my prayer warrior. I, who had been too blinded by selfish pride, had been unable to see that before. But now I do.

An All Wise God of Grace

It was a gracious, loving, patient God who designed every detail of my life that I might grow in His grace, His love and His forgiveness.

2 Corinthians 4:6-11

For God, who commanded the light to shine out of darkness, hath shined in our hearts, to give the light of the knowledge of the Glory of God in the face of Jesus Christ. But we have this treasure in earthen vessels, that the excellency of the power may be of God, and not of us.

We are troubled on every side, yet not distressed; we are perplexed, but not in despair; Persecuted, but not forsaken; cast down, but not destroyed; Always bearing about in the body the dying of the Lord Jesus, that the life also of Jesus might be made manifest in our body.

For we which live are always delivered unto death for Jesus' sake, that the life also of Jesus might be made manifest in our mortal flesh.

Whatever you are facing today, know this: God is using every detail in your life to transform you into the image of Christ. He is patiently, gently, lovingly chiseling away the stony parts of your heart that you might know the truth of love and forgiveness in Christ Jesus.

Learning to Loving like Jesus

God is love. Throughout my life, I searched for love. That took me through many stages as I learned. By nature, we are born with a great need to love and be loved. However, sin leaves us with stony hearts that must be transformed before we can be truly loving like Jesus. A lesson that often takes a lifetime to learn. From the moment one accepts Jesus as Savior and Lord, His power indwells us in the form of the Holy Spirit. Yet, His spirit of love cannot shine forth through the stony fortress around our hearts. As young, helpless babies need to be cared for and need to be loved, at first incapable of truly loving in return, so are we. The task of transforming us into the image of Jesus Christ, God takes on as His mission for each of those who accept His gift of salvation through Jesus Christ.

With great skill, the Master Surgeon chips away at the stony edges of our heart. At times, we feel our hearts break. Yet, with gentle and loving skill, God wraps His loving hands around the broken areas. He opens areas where His light of love can shine forth to the world around us. Through many stages of love, we must walk to be transformed from need love to being able to truly love. We face many forms of love-from friendship love, familial love, and Eros. Each stage for the believer, God uses to transform our hearts, so we may become loving like Jesus loves.

My love for Mom was so combined with my need love that I could not see clearly until God had taught me further lessons of love in other areas of my life. What a wise, patient and gentle teacher He has been. Loving like Jesus is an impossible task for our hearts without God's guiding hand transforming us first.

5 lessons from God On Love

1. Before I can become loving like Jesus, I must first comprehend His depth of love for me. Perhaps at times this seems to be the hardest of tasks; because, my sin nature wants to feel validated in that love. In other words, I want to feel deserving of that love. Yet, the truth is: I am not. Were it not for His pursuing me, I would not by nature ever desire Him, although He is the greatest treasure and so worthy to be desired! He fought for me, He died for me, and He longs that I comprehend His abounding love for me.

    All that He desires is to bring me to that place of abiding, steadfast joy in Him. There is no other love that can fully satisfy the longing of my heart, though I search for it diligently in other counterfeit loves and joys. All else this world could offer would have left me further broken, were it not for His love which reached out to save me.

    "That Christ may dwell in your hearts by faith; that ye, being rooted and grounded in love, may be able to comprehend with all saints what is the breadth, and length, and depth, and height; and to know the love of

Christ, which passeth knowledge, that ye might be filled with all the fulness of God" (Ephesians 3:17-19)

2. I must come to realize that without Him, I can never become truly loving like Jesus. My heart sees only my desires to be loved. The center of my universe, by nature, is me and all else falls into the categories of how the world around me makes me feel. That is the case with every human heart without God. Our self-centeredness interferes with our ability to see or know truth. Then mistakenly, truth becomes what I, emotionally believe it to be. Yet, that cannot be reality.

    If I see a light streaking across the night sky and believe it to be a falling star. Another may see the same light and believes it to be an airplane's light. Only one of us is right. Truth demands that only one is true and that comes from outside of us, not just what we believe to be true. God is truth.

    "He is the rock, his work is perfect: for all His ways are judgment: A God of truth, without iniquity, just and right is He" (Deuteronomy 32:4).

    For me to learn of the truth of love, I must learn God's truth. I must learn to see the world through His eyes, if I seek to know truth. Only then, can I be loving like Jesus.

3. Learning of God's love for me and my inability to truly love with a Christ like love, then I trust Him to transform my heart. Whatever it takes, I trust His wisdom. Even when storms and trials come, I understand that He is busy transforming my stony heart into one into one of love. He will perfect us in loving like Jesus.

"I (God) will give you one heart and a new spirit; I will take from you your hearts of stone and give you tender hearts of love for God" (Ezekiel 11:19 TLB)[21]

Jesus prayed, *"And the glory which thou gavest me I have given them; that they may be one, even as we are one: I in them, and thou in me, that they may be made perfect in one; and that the world may know that thou has sent me, and hast love them, as thou hast love me"* John 17:22-23).

4. To be perfected in love, we must know and follow His commands. That we do, as we study His word, grow in our knowledge of Him. He does the work within us as we trust in Him, spend time with Him through studying His love letters (the Bible), pray, and allow Him to transform us from the inside out.

"But whoso keepeth His word, in Him verily is the love of God perfected: hereby know we that we are in Him" (I John 2:5).

It is not I then; but, Christ in me that is my hope of loving like Christ with a perfect love. Laying aside all of who I am that He might live in me. I die to self, that He might live and only then, do I truly live

5. Study and learn what love truly is as He laid out so beautifully in 1 Corinthians 13 and in the life of Jesus. We will address 1 Corinthians 13 in the next chapter.

WHISPERS OF LOVE

Whispers of Love flowing all through my life

Even in moments of sorrow or strife

Whispers that came in the dark of the night

Promising Joy with the new morning light

Whispers of hope for the bleakest of day

"Love will find strength and will find its way"

Into your heart and grow from within

Until it flows forth rejoicing and then

Suddenly out of those long and sad years

Love does spring forth out of fountains of tears

Into rivers of joy bursting forth then to see

That love had been there abiding in me

Oh, thank you dear Lord for teaching me love

As Your spirit descends with the wings of a dove

And gathered the pieces of this shattered heart

To weave it with steel, Your glory impart

A Picture so rare, its beauty unmasked

A portrait of you made in brilliant stained glass

Your love had been there inside of me

Even when I had been too blind to see

Whispers of love, it was You all along

Holding me close, I am your love song!

Chapter 9:

Agape Love, A Worthwhile Costly Love

Having accepted Jesus Christ as my Savior and Lord, I am adopted into the family of God. He, being the loving Father that He is, desires that I fully reap the blessings of being His child. As such, God recognizes my heart needs to be transformed. Outside adornment of Christ's righteous robes affords me His presence. However, underneath those robes I have a stony heart requiring transformation. When I accepted God's gift of salvation through faith in Jesus Christ, I immediately was hidden in Christ. Furthermore, I was given a helper, the Holy Spirit. His task is to transform me into the image of Christ, perfecting me both in righteousness and love. Not a simple task; but, one He will complete; whatever it takes. One day, my heart will love like God does with an Agape Love.

Yet, what does Agape Love really look like? It is the love of God, the Father for His Son and the Son for His Father outflowing, encircling and abounding within the Holy Spirit. Furthermore, scripture tells us in John 17:23, God saw through the corridors of time and knew each one who would come to know Him through faith and loved each one with the same love that Father and Son experienced together. Imagine that! God loves me with the same love as He loved His perfect, righteous son. However, He does not stop there. He paid the price that I might be brought into His family where His love could shower His blessings upon me. I am not referring to material blessings here. But I am referring to blessings far greater: that of love, joy, hope and peace in Him and through Him.

Agape Love

We are given an idea of what agape love looks like in I Corinthians 13:4-7 (TLB)[22]

Love is very patient and kind, never jealous or envious, never boastful or proud, never haughty or selfish or rude. Love does not demand its own way. It is not irritable or touchy. It does not hold grudges and will hardly even notice when others do it wrong. It is never glad about injustice but rejoices whenever truth wins out. If you love someone, you will be loyal to him (or her) no matter what the cost. You will always believe in him (or her), always expect (believe) the best of him (or her), and always stand your ground in defending him (or her).

Although a very popular scripture for weddings, how many can truly love with agape love. We fall so far short. At least, I know my self-exalting human heart cannot. My only hope to love with the slightest resemblance of this, is to die to my own selfish desires that God's love might shine through me. I must take up my cross daily, dying to self that He might live. And this, I cannot do without His doing it for me. He must through whatever means necessary slay the dragon of selfish pride within my heart and chip away the stony walls surrounding my heart to transform it.

Through Sorrows and Pains to Abiding Steadfast Joy

Through trials, pains, suffering and brokenness we are transformed into the image of Christ. Yet, it is worth every tear, scar, and despairing moment; because, as we learn to love God, trusting Him, we find in Him an abiding, steadfast joy that lifts us above all the circumstances of this life. We can see Jesus Christ, in the face of eternity. Therefore, we labor on.

Thank God, He did not leave me where He found me clothed in my filthy rags of self-righteousness, buried in my stony grave of counterfeit love. Instead, He chose to transform me. Oh, He is not done with transforming me yet; but neither am I where I began. He loved me too much to leave me there. God saw what I could become, believed in what He could transform me into, and was willing to stand beside me no matter what. What about you? Do you know Him? If so, prepare yourself for the greatest adventure of life, more than you could ever imagine.

Is True Love Always a Costly Love?

If indeed we are to love as Jesus loved, we will pay a price as well. For the truest of loves, is a costly love. It willingly lays aside all selfish desire for the good of the beloved. Always seeking their needs, their enrichment, and laying aside our own. Oh, there are moments perhaps that we humans can achieve that. However, always? That requires

213

more than this human heart can achieve in its own strength. Yet, Jesus Christ demonstrated for us what a costly love looks like. Furthermore, He has promised to be there in us to guide us to that place of perfect love in Him and through His mighty power within us. Beyond that, He has promised that despite all the pain, sorrow and suffering that true love may bring, it is worth it in the end; because, of the joy that we shall find there.

What Is Costly Love?

We all understand what C. S. Lewis ascribes in His book *The Four Loves* regarding the vulnerability and pain love may bring. Regarding love,

"There is no safe investment. To love at all is to be vulnerable. Love anything and your heart will certainly be wrung and possibly be broken. If you want to make sure of keeping it intact, you must give your heart to no one, not even to an animal. Wrap it carefully round with hobbies and little luxuries; avoid all entanglements; lock it up safe in the casket or coffin of your selfishness.

But in that casket-safe, dark, motionless, airless—it will change. It will not be broken; it will become unbreakable, impenetrable, irredeemable. The alternative to tragedy, or at least to the risk of tragedy, is damnation. The only place outside Heaven where you can be perfectly safe from all the dangers and perturbations of love is Hell."[23]

Certainly, we would consider that costly love; because our hearts can be vulnerable and thereby breakable. But what I mean by costly love goes much further than that.

The True Cost of Costly Love

To love like Christ loves, as we are commanded to in John 13:34. "*A new commandment I give unto you, that ye love one another; as I have loved you, that ye also love one another.*"

---

[23] C.S. Lewis, *The Four Loves,* (1960), in *The Beloved Works of C.S. Lewis,* (Edison, NJ: Inspirational Press, 2004)., 278-279.

How did Christ love? If we are to imitate Him, we must see how He loved the apostles to whom He spoke. He loved them when they were foolish, the same as when they got it right. (More often were they foolish than right). He ever so gently guided them to see and know the truth. Patiently, gently He cared for them; although, He knew perfectly when to allow them to stumble that they might learn to walk boldly. Furthermore, He humbly served them, never placing His physical needs above theirs. He loved them when they were at their worst and with compassion guided them to become their best in Him, through faith. Also, He lived the example for them both in His devotion to prayer and obedience to the Father.

Then, came the ultimate act of costly love. He died that they might be saved. Bearing the full brunt of the penalty due us, He laid down His life that we might gain ours. *"For scarcely for a righteous man will one die: yet peradventure for a good man some would even dare to die. But God commandeth His love toward us, in that, while we were yet*

sinners, Christ died for us. Much more then, being now

justified by His blood, we shall be saved from wrath through

Him" (Romans 5:7-9).

We are also commanded to *"take up our cross daily*

to follow Him" (Luke 9:23). Our cross is to die to self, that

He might live through us. God desires to "perfect" us in love.

The Greatest Treasure to be Found

Dying to self is the only way to learn to truly love.

Indeed, true love is a costly love; however, it is so worth

finding. Only there can we rise above the circumstances and

trials of this life, to soar on wings like eagles with God's breath

supporting and guiding our flight. Therein, we find His

abiding, steadfast joy no matter how difficult the circumstance

or how fragile our hearts may feel. Then, one day when we

stand before Him, we will know just how great a treasure we

have found.

"When we see the face of God, we shall know that we have always known it. He has been a party to, has made, sustained and moved moment by moment within, all our earthly experiences of innocent love. All that was true love in them was, even on earth, far more His than ours, and ours only because His. In Heaven there will be no anguish and no duty of turning away from our earthly Beloveds. First, because we shall have turned already; from the portraits to the Original, from the rivulets to the Fountain, from the creatures He made loveable to Love Himself. But secondly, because we shall find them all in Him. By loving Him more than them we shall love them more than we now do." C. S. Lewis[24]

Ah, but I daresay the same is true here on earth. I cannot truly love another with a Christ like love; until, I grasp the truth of God's love. Yes, true love is a costly love; but it is well worth the cost-whatever that may be.

----

[24] C.S. Lewis, *The Four Loves,* (1960), in *The Beloved Works of C.S. Lewis,* (Edison, NJ: Inspirational Press, 2004)., 288.

To Love God

As I often remind myself and you, faith is knowing God IS and that He is a rewarder of those who diligently seek Him. Our faith and our ability to love Him falters on both truths all too often. We either do not fully believe that He is the Almighty, Sovereign God of the universe or we falter in believing He really, truly loves us. If we truly believed both truths in the depth of our hearts and being, we would be incapable of not demonstrating our love for Him through trusting Him, joyfully seeking to be in His presence, and resting fully in His Sovereign Grace. So, how can we truly love God with all our heart, our mind and our strength?

When questioned concerning the commandments, Jesus answered, "*The first of all the commandments is...The Lord our God is one Lord: And thou shalt love the Lord thy God with all thy heart, and will all thy soul, and will all thy mind, and with all thy strength: this is the first commandment,*

And the second is like, namely this, Thou shalt love thy neighbour as thyself" (Mark 12:29-31).

The whole point is we cannot love our family, our friends, or our neighbors unless we first learn to love God with all our heart, soul, mind and strength. But what does "to love God" look like?

To Love God with All Your Heart

How does one love God with all their heart? This is referring to the central core of one's being. Understanding that true "being" is only found in Him, without whom only nothingness exists. *"For in Him we live, and move, and have our being"* (Acts 17:28). To love God with all your heart also means to trust Him with every detail of your life. Amid your darkest night, you trust His love, rest in knowing He is Sovereign, and that He is executing the best plan for your life. His desire for you is that you are wrapped in His love, enveloped in His Joy and heir of His Glory.

Only He can see all the future as well as the present. He knows precisely what is needed to prepare your heart, mind and soul to truly live life to its fullest with abiding, steadfast abounding joy. Also, He is constantly about the process of transforming your heart to maximally rejoice in Him eternally in His presence.

Love God with all your soul

The soul is the consciousness of mankind, that which is eternal. *"And the Lord God formed man of the dust of the ground and breathed into his nostrils the breath of life; and man became a living soul"* (Genesis 2:7). This is what separated humans from the animal kingdom. We have a consciousness and a conscience that remains eternal. Recognizing this to be true, that man was more than this fleshly body, is what lead a lifelong atheist such as Jean Paul Sartre to recognize God's existence on his dying bed as he proclaimed: "I do not feel that I am the product of chance, a speck of dust in the universe, but someone who was expected, prepared, prefigured. In short a being only a Creator could put here; and this idea of a creating hand refers to God."[25]

So, to love God with all your soul is to consciously be aware of His continuous presence in your life. Furthermore, it is recognizing that there is not a thought, idea, word or deed that one can perform outside of God's watchful eye. That should certainly be a sobering thought.

Psalm 139:1-13

O Lord, thou hast searched me, and known me. Thou knowest my downsitting and min uprising, thou understandest my thought afar off. Thou compassest my path and my lying down, and art acquainted with all my ways. For there is not a word in my tongue, but, lo, O Lord, thou knowest it altogether. Thou hast beset me behind and before and laid thine hand upon me.

---

[25] Ravi Zacharias, *The End of Reason,* (Grand Rapids, MI: Zondervan, 2008),43.

Such knowledge is too wonderful for me; it is high, I cannot attain unto it. Whither shall I go from thy spirit? Or whither shall I flee from thy presence?

If I ascend up into heaven, thou art there: if I make my bed in hell, behold thou art there. If I take the wings of the morning, and dwell in the uttermost parts of the sea; Even there shall thy hand lead me, and thy right hand shall hold me.

If I say, Surely the darkness shall cover me; even the night shall be light about me. Yea, the darkness hideth not from thee; but the night shineth as the day: the darkness and the light are both alike to thee. For thou has possessed my reins.

To Love God with All Your Mind

Our mind can easily be filled with the events of our day. Entertainment, work, chores, music, friends, bills, questions, choices and the lists go on. Needless to say, our minds are bombarded with ideas. So, how do we live life and at the same time love God with all our mind? It boils down to some of our choices. Either for entertainment or music, I can choose to listen to that which feeds my mind with secular ideologies or that which feeds my mind with worship. I have found that the more I occupy my mind with Him, the easier all the tasks at work or home go. I can listen to worship music in the background, which settles my restless brain and helps me to focus on the task at hand.

On the other hand, when I fill my mind with useless entertainment, I find myself growing restless and unfocused in everything else. Doubt grows, fear expands, and everything else becomes an impossible task.

To Love God with all your strength

This perhaps is the most curious, "*for when I am weak then am I strong*" (2 Corinthians 12:10). When I surrender all of who I am, then, I love God with all my strength. His strength in me to perform what I could not on my own. Following His commandments by the strength of His Holy

Spirit empowering me to do so. Obedience is an expression of loving God with all your strength. That obedience can only come with the help of the Holy Spirit indwelling us. Then all my strength is His strength in me and not really mine at all.

How to Find Rest in a Sovereign God of Love

There was a time when I questioned, "Why, Lord?" Why did Mom suffer so from her bipolar disease? What could have been the purpose of Pete's suffering? To the world, it appeared that this horrid disease won. But you see, it did not. What if every sorrow, tear, or pain leads to one finding eternal rest in the arms of a Sovereign God of love? Then, wasn't it worth every sorrow, tear, or pain traversed along this road of life! God knows each heart. He knows precisely what is needed to lead one to Christ's eternal joy. Beyond that He willingly bore our pain and sorrows as well.

A Sovereign God of Love Wept

The shortest verse in the Bible is "Jesus Wept" (John 11:35). So, often we hear preachers teach that therein Jesus wept over the death of his friend Lazarus. And that He wept because He felt the sorrow of all of those around Him. Yet, as Ken Davis pointed out in "*It's Enough to Make A Grown Man Cry*", Jesus knew that He would raise Lazarus from the dead. Therefore, He wept because His disciples could not see the full truth. He is the greatest treasure and not even death could separate a believer from Him. He, the Sovereign God of Love, was and is eternal life to all who believe. We can trust fully in Him and rest in that truth. Every detail of our life, He is in control and only He can see the final portrait.

Each tear we shed. The fears, sorrows, and pains we face all are a part of fulfilling His Divine purpose in our life. He is using each thread to form a tapestry of great beauty-a portrait of God's only son. A Sovereign God of Love knows precisely what is needed to transform each heart into one that

226

can fully trust in and rejoice in Him for all of eternity. This life is but a blink in time compared to eternity. Jesus wept because His friends and disciples could not fully comprehend the truth: they could rest and find joy even in their sorrow because of Him. Therefore, they could rejoice even in their sorrow; because the Sovereign God of love was and is still on His throne. Oh, how it must pain God each time I anxiously wonder in fear asking, "Why, Lord?" instead of trusting Him. I am certain that Jesus has wept each time I doubted His plan.

Lesson from God in a Bipolar World

Mom's illness prepared me to be Pedro Barba's wife. God miraculously used those years I lived with Pete to bring Him to a saving knowledge of Jesus Christ. I say miraculously because as I see it, I failed so often; but God used me anyway despite my weakness and frailty. Not that He needed me; but that He graciously gave me the opportunity to be one of the vessels He used to bring Pete to Himself. Every thread of my life, mom's life, and Pete's pointing to a Sovereign God of love, who knew our hearts. Which brings me to rejoice in Him. The greatest way I can demonstrate my love toward Him is to trust Him every day, no matter what comes. I can fully trust in His plans. He only wants what is best for me. My darkest valleys only bring me closer to Him.

When all the world enwraps me in darkness, He is my light. He gives to me His Abiding, Steadfast Joy to walk through my hardest trials. Then, I can proclaim as David.

PSALM 139:14-18,23-14

I will praise thee; for I am fearfully and wonderfully made: marvelous are thy works; and that my soul knoweth right well. My substance was not hid from thee, when I was made in secret, and curiously wrought in the lowest part of the earth. Thine eyes did see my substance yet being unperfect; and in thy book all my members were written, which in continuance were fashioned, when as yet there was none of them. How precious also are thy thoughts unto me, O God! How great is the sum of them! If I should count them, they are more in number than the sand: when I awake, I am still with thee...Search me, O God, and know my heart: try me, and know my thoughts: And see if there be any wicked way in me, and lead me in the way everlasting.

Then can I proclaim, "Whatever it takes Lord, help me to see You clearer each day. Make me into a reflection of You. Oh, Sovereign God of love, empty me of myself, that I might be a life saving vessel to a world in need of You.

GOD'S PLAN OF LOVE

Oh, Love Divine, what greater thought
That you should suffer, bleed and die
To pay my sin, my freedom bought
Though I screamed Crucify
With every action of my life
I cast aside your pleading cries
I caused you pain, I gave you strife
And chose to follow after lies
I could not see your beauty then
As now I see your face
Your light shone forth, e'er so dim
That I might see Your Grace
You drew me out, you pulled me in
That I might then seek you
You covered then my ugly sin
Your righteousness to view
Such love Divine, pursuing me
Your Joy and Hope to share
How could I run, How could I flee
Naught else could e'er compare
Unto the hope I find in You
As now I turn to seek your Face
Your Glory shines and lights my view
You guide me on at gentle pace
Transforming thus my wretched heart
Unto the one You knew I'd be
Your joyous love ne'er to depart
For all eternity.

TO GOD-MY LOVE, MY HOPE, MY JOY

My life-so filled with hopes and dreams

Lay shattered at Your feet

So many tears, so many pains

I laid before Your seat

Can I look upon Your face of love

And question what You've done?

For You have been my only hope

My only morning sun

You've seen my heart when crushed with pain

Your hands have held it tight

When I have been so weak, so frail

You've shown Your strength, Your might

You've held me close within Your arms

When darkness filled my night

And when I could not see my way

Your eyes, they gave me sight

I lay my life within Your hands

That You may heal my soul

And keep my eyes upon You Lord

That I may reach Your goal

Shine forth Your grace, Your mercy Lord

And let me be Your light

That all may see Your eyes of love

The blind, they might have sight

Let not the sorrows, nor the pains

Bring bitterness within

And give me strength to walk this path

Protect my heart from sin

I lay my heart, my soul, my dreams

Before Your throne of love

I lift my eyes to You, My God

And seek Your will above

You are the only one I need

To fill my heart with glee

It is Your face, my one true love

Tis all I need to see

So lift me up and hold me close

Reveal Your love divine

That through the holes within my heart

A world might see You shine

And if the sorrows of my past

Can touch a wayward one

I thank you Lord for each dark path

That lead them to Your son

I praise You now from mountains high

For each dark path I've trod

Twas there I found Your heart, Your love

Twas there I found You God

What great and wondrous joy I know

Because You are my king

And though the path I cannot see

My heart will trust and sing

A song of praise unto You Lord

Who knows what's best for me

You'll hold my hand and lead me on

In darkness, I can see

Your love, Your help, Your guiding hand

Is all I'll ever need

So hold me close unto Your path

For this is all I plead

I'll skip with joy along this path

Though darkness may surround

Because I know You hold my hand

My feet will ne'er touch ground

I cannot fall outside Your love

I cannot lose my way

I'll hold my broken dreams once more

And see them real, one day

A song of praise unto You Lord

Who knows what's best for me

You'll hold my hand and lead me on

In darkness, I can see

Your love, Your help, Your guiding hand

Is all I'll ever need

So hold me close unto Your path

For this is all I plead

Works Cited

Augustine. *Enchiridion on Faith, Hope, and Love.* Translated by J.F. Shaw. Chicago: Henry Reguery, 1961.

Edwards, Jonathan. "Concerning the Divine Decrees." In *The Works of Jonathan Edwards.* Edinburgh, Scotland: Banner of Truth, 1974.

"Jealous." *google.com/dictionary.* July 11, 2018. https://www.google.com/search?q=Dictionary#dobs=jealous .

Kierkegaard. *the Sickness unto Death.* Translated by Alastair Hannay. London: Penquin Books, 2004.

Kierkegaard, Soren. *The Gospel of Sufferings.* Translated by A. S. Aldworth and W. S. Ferrie. Cambridge, United Kingdom: James Clarke & Co., 1955.

Labyrinth. "Jealous." *Google.com/lyrics.* July 11, 2018. https://www.google.com/search?q=lyrics+to+jealous+by+labrinth&oq=lyrics+to+jealous&aqs=chrome.1.69i57j0l5.13780j1j7&sourceid=chrome&ie=UTF-8 .

Lewis, C.S. *Mere Christianity.* New York: Macmillan, 1952.

Lloyd-Jones, D. Martyn. *Spiritual Depression It's Causes and Cure.* Grand Rapids, MI: Wm. B. Eerdman Publishing, 1965.

Newton, John and William Cowper. *Olney Hymns.* London, England: St. Pauls Churchyard, 1797.

Zacharias, Ravi. *Cries of the Heart.* Nashville, TN: W Publishing Group, 2002.